El Camino de Santi

The Camino Franc
St. Jean-Pied-de-Port to Santiago de Compostela

*To Nicola with all best wishes for your own writing –*

*[signature]*

# A Personal Pilgrimage

May 16th to June 21st 2003
Walking in the footsteps of William de Mohun,
an ancestor, who walked this way in 1280 AD

by Michael G. Moon

Some historical facts and legends about the 'Camino de Santiago'.

Santiago is the Spanish city named after Saint Iago (Saint James)

James, son of Zeberdee, was the fisherman who became the 4th Apostle of Christ. It is said that he came to Spain to preach the gospel, but returned to Jerusalem in AD44 and was martyred (beheaded) by Herod Agrippa.

Legend has it that his remains were then mysteriously returned to Spain by two of his followers in a stone boat, without sails or oars, which drifted ashore on the Galician coast near Padron. Permission was given for the burial of the remains in a field on a hilltop, some 16km inland.

Some eight hundred years later! A hermit saw a strange light or star which revealed the Apostle's burial place. The name Compostela, derives from either Compostium (burial place) or campos stellae (starry field). You can take your choice. A church was constructed on the site which was then called Santiago de Compostela.

From this point on (844AD), St. James (St. Iago) became a focal point in Spanish history. Santiago became a pilgrim destination ranking in importance with Rome and Jerusalem. An 11th century papal decree granted pilgrims full or partial indulgence (forgiveness) of their sins in return for their suffering and penitence while traversing the hazardous routes across Europe, to touch the relics of the Apostle.

The Camino means 'The Way' and is synonymous with the various pilgrim routes to Santiago. The huge popularity of the pilgrimage resulted in the passage of millions of pilgrims throughout the middle ages. They opened up Northern Iberia after centuries of neglect and isolation, bringing new ideas, commerce and culture.

St. Iago was also used as the rallying symbol for the re-conquest of Muslim Spain. He appeared to King Ramiro, before the battle at Clavijo in Rioja. Astride a white charger and wielding a shining sword, the image of St Iago led the Christian army in the first successful counter offensive against Islam in Spain. St. Iago took on the new title of Santiago Matamoros (The Moorslayer) and as such became the figurehead for the long campaign leading to the total Christian re-conquest in 1492.

St. Iago, is also portrayed as a pilgrim or 'pelegrino' in his own right, standing as an example of achieving salvation through penitence and suffering. The scallop shell symbol probably dates back to St. James' humble beginnings as a fisherman. There is however a colourful story that when his remains were being brought ashore at Padron, a horseman plunged into the sea beside the stone boat and emerged covered in scallop shells. Whatever the truth the scallop shell is one of the constant and defining images of the camino.

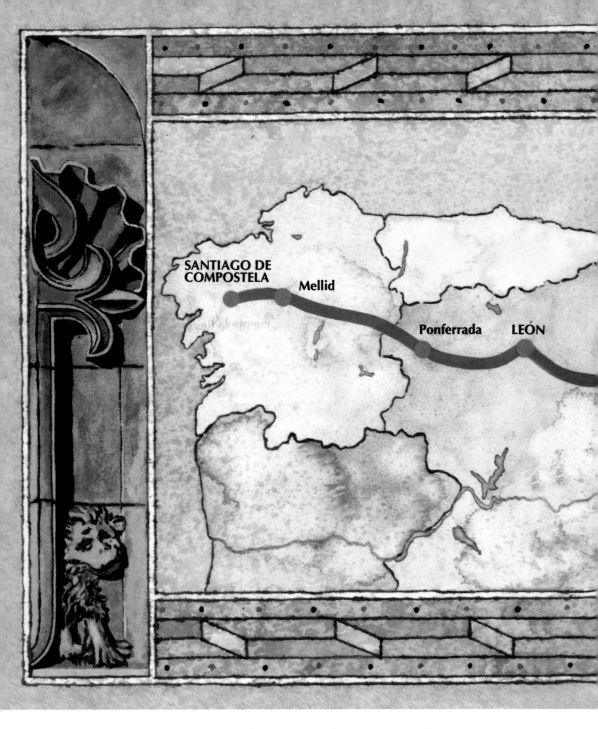

SANTIAGO DE
COMPOSTELA

Mellid

Ponferrada    LEÓN

This is a map of 'The Camino de Santiago'. There are several routes eminating
from France but the one I chose was from St. Jean-Pied-de-Port and is known
as the 'Camino Francais'. I was captivated by the idea of walking into Spain in
the footsteps of Charlemagne and Napoleon. The whole route across Northern

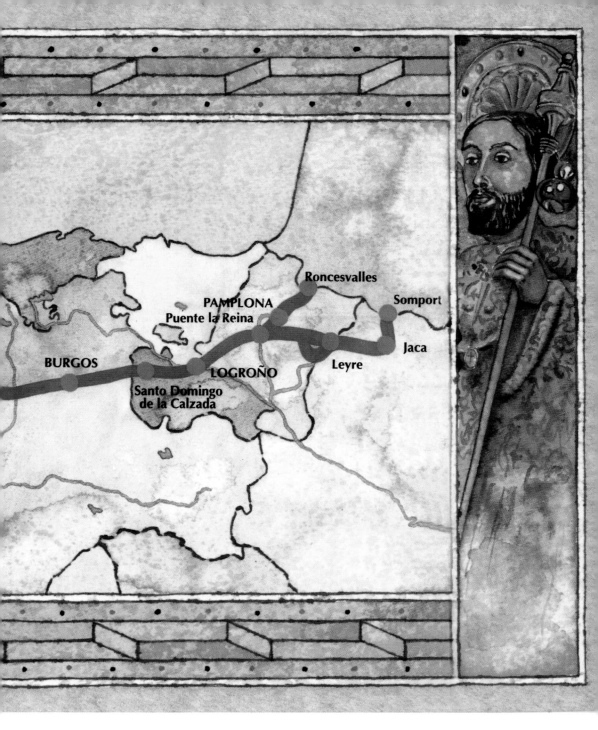

Spain is magnificent in terms of scenery, history, architecture, food and wine. Whether you are walking to save your soul, raise your spirit or simply stretch your legs then 'The Camino' is the way to go.

# Introduction

*I am not certain when exactly I first heard about*
*the pilgrims way to Camino de Santiago,*
*but as soon as I read about it I knew,*
*instinctively, that it was something that*
**I had to do!**

I tucked the idea away in my mind for a few years and then, when real retirement (I had already retired twice), seemed inevitable, I started to consider it seriously. I read up some accounts of the pilgrimage and its history, looked at maps and discovered the Confraternity of St. James in London as the source of up to date information and suppliers of help, support and encouragement.

I am not a Catholic and, in truth, not at all certain of my real faith. I accept the neccessity for the moral codes, which seem to be shared by all major religions, but I have difficulty in understanding how the bloody conflicts and repressions that have continually riven the world can be conducted in the name of religion and true faith. I also have difficulty in reconciling the huge wealth and power of the churches of most religions, often manifest in the magnificence of their structures and artefacts, with the abject poverty of large sections of their followers.

It might seem strange therefore that I should be drawn to undertake a pilgrimage that embodies the combative and bloody history of religious wars and the wealth and power of the Catholic church in Spain.

My main motivation initially was simply to do a long walk through an interesting area with a nice climate and have the chance to think through what I was going to do with the rest of my life.

The more I read about the Camino de Santiago however, and the accounts of previous and current pilgrims, it became apparent that there is something special about the experience. The history, the varied terrain of Northern Spain, the architecture, the myths and legends, the camaraderie of the pilgrims and, not least, the fact that they (pilgrims) have been walking over the same route for some 1,000 years, often enduring danger, suffering and death, to expatiate their sins and ensure their place in heaven.

Despite having finally retired in 2002, I had, for various reasons, put off the 'Camino'. Then two things happened that brought it to the top of my 'things to do' list.

The first was an extraordinary discovery. I was finally, having time available, undertaking another major project researching and compiling my family history.

The family of De Mohun (Moon) had come over with William the Conqueror and had been a very prominent family in the West Country with major landholdings in Somerset, Dorset, Devon and Cornwall. While reading one of the many publications on the family, I came across the amazing fact that Sir William de Mohun of Mohuns Ottery in Devon (still inhabited today) had completed a pilgrimage to Santiago in 1280. I was able to verify this through The Calendar of Patent Rolls at the National Archives.

The fact that an ancestor had also determined to take the same pilgrimage some 700 years ago seemed to me to be a clear sign that my own pilgrimage was, in some way, predestined.

On a more mundane, but in some ways more important level, I now also needed to re-evaluate my own life. I had not found retirement particularly easy. I needed to take stock and set some fresh goals. I was reluctant to settle for comfortable old age and yet uncertain as to how I could balance personal ambitions with changing family needs. I needed the time and space to think things through.

These two factors suddenly made the pilgrimage at once imperative and much more significant than a nice stroll across Northern Spain.

In the autumn of 2002, I visited the Confraternity of St. James in London and purchased their 'Pilgrims Guide' to the Camino Frances, acknowledged as the best guide available and kept up to date annually. I reread all my notes, had a medical, attended my local gym, and started doing some walking in the local hills. With the aid of the Confraternity guide I went shopping and purchased all my equipment.

I decided that May/June would be the best timeframe both from convenience and weather and booked a one-way ticket to Barcelona for the 13th of May 2003.

The following is a summary of my diary, recollections and thoughts on the journey to Santiago de Compostella.

# 13th of May, Tuesday.
# Liverpool to Pamplona.

A good friend took me to Liverpool Airport. He lifted out my rucksack from the boot of his car and was very dubious that I would be able to carry it to the check in desk, let alone 500 miles across Northern Spain. I was not sure that I would be able to myself, but I had reduced the contents to what I thought was the absolute minimum. I realised later that my minimum could be reduced by at least another 50%.

The flight to Barcelona by Easyjet went very smoothly although delayed by an hour because of the inevitable French Air Traffic Control strike.

At Barcelona Airport, I picked up a hire car that I could return to Pamplona Airport the following evening.

I drove the 350km to Pamplona in one day, brilliant roads, virtually traffic free. Not a lot to see initially except miles and miles of flat plains and further north some amazing rock formations. After Zaragoza, everything became greener and hillier with views of the Pyrenees beginning to dominate the horizon.

Drove round and round the centre of Pamplona looking for somewhere to park. Found a small central hotel, Hotel Avenida. Very good value.

I explored Old Pamplona in the early evening. A lovely city. Would be a good place to stay and explore this end of the Pyrenees.

It is the capital of Navarre and perhaps most famous for the Bull Run round the Plaza del Castillo. Unfortunately the plaza is mainly closed off as they are putting a car park underneath it! However I went round the Cathedral de Santa Maria with a marvellous interior and the Museo de Navarra with some great Spanish art including a Goya.

Had dinner at the hotel.

The plan for tomorrow is to drive to St. Jean-Pied-de-Port following the Camino route where possible, book up my first night's accommodation in St. Jean, do a little exploring and then drive back and return the car to Pamplona Airport in the evening.

Well I am here, footloose, and to a degree, fancy free. It does feel good to be on my own with a clear goal in front of me and a simple task of walking west every morning. I am going to do my best to put everything out of my mind for a few days and just concentrate on getting the walking started and getting acclimatised to the idea of being a pilgrim.

# 14th of May, Wednesday.
# Drive from Pamplona to
# St. Jean-Pied-de-Port and back.

Set off from Pamplona at about 10.00am after coffee and a danish. It was a fantastic drive with empty roads through the mountains. The villages are very Swiss in appearance, white painted chalets with shutters, green fields in the valleys with beautiful creamy brown cows.

Reached St. Jean at about 1.00pm and visited the house of the Acceuil St. Jacques, who were very helpful and recommended a B&B as the refugio is completely full. They also provided a detailed sketch plan of both the road and mountain route to Roncesvalles. I went to the B&B, Maison E Bernat, at 20 Rue de la Citadelle, and made a reservation for tomorrow night.

Had a brilliant French lunch in the sun at the Hotel Central, looking down on a river full of trout. Basque omelette, veal escalope with frites and a green salad, crème caramel to die for and French coffee washed down with half a bottle of local wine (18 euros). Probably the last civilised meal for a while.

Good drive back to Pamplona. Gave a lift to two Frenchmen, academics who were walking part of the Camino but were running out of time and needed to get a lift into Pamplona. They were very appreciative.

Returned the car to the airport. Quiet night in. Arranged for a taxi in the morning, from a local taxi driver, Francisco, as recommended by the Confraternity of St. James in London.

Excellent day. I have seen the start of the route. The mountains look a bit intimidating but also exciting and just fantastic scenery. I am looking forward to actually starting the walk. I feel ready for it. I am still not sure whether to go the road route or the route Napoleon, via the Col de Lepoeder, over the mountains. Common sense says the road route, but my heart says that I will regret it if I don't accept the challenge of the route Napoleon. I wonder which way William de Mohun chose?

# 15th of May, Thursday.
# Taxi to St. Jean-Pied-de-Port.

Up at 7.30am. Repacked my rucksack. Coffee and croissant in hotel coffee shop. Posted hire car documents to Europcar (I forgot to leave them yesterday). Francisco turned up on time. No English so rather limited conversation in fractured French. Very friendly. Stopped en route at his sister's house in Burguete so that he could copy a plan of the route that he had, which he then gave to me, marking most of the refugios and small pensions/hotels.

Arrived in St. Jean at about 12.00pm. Checked into the B&B and met Monsieur. and Madame Bernat, very charming and hospitable. They have a restaurant attached to the B&B, so I booked in for dinner this evening. Madame Bernat also said they would make me a picnic lunch to take with me tomorrow.

Had a snack lunch, walked round the very imposing citadel. Walking through the old gate to the town gave a real sense of deja vu. Very nice little town, definitely a good starting point. I also walked a couple of miles out of town on the route I will need to take tomorrow. It certainly looks steep. Visited the church, very pretty and peaceful. Lit a candle for ma and pa. I think they would be quite pleased about this pilgrimage. Bought some water for tomorrow, as shops will not be open when I start out and there are no shops on the route. Had a bath and washed my clothes.

Excellent dinner. The restaurant was small but full of locals. Had trout pate and something called Aoxa. Don't know what it was but delicious, followed by Basque cherry tarte. Should sleep well.

*Sign on the gate of 'Les Amis du Chemin de St. Jacques'.*

*Mountains near to the Col de Lepoeder. The way to go?*

I am really ready to get going now. A bit apprehensive about my pack, rather wish I had practised walking with it fully loaded, it does feel very heavy. It's too late now. I am still undecided about which route to take tomorrow. I will see what the weather is like in the morning.

## 16th of May, Friday.
## St. Jean-Pied-de-Port to
## Roncesvalles. 26km.

I am walking!!

Slept very well. Alarm at 6.30am. Breakfast at 7.00am, started out at 7.30am. Beautiful morning, decided finally, despite the warnings, to do the route Napoleon to Roncesvalles and make up a day.

The start was tough. Very steep initial climb out of St. Jean. Only saw one pilgrim, who turned out as I passed him, to be German. He was dressed in a robe and reading prayers aloud as he walked. A true pilgrim!

The climb was relentless. Up and up and up. Good road surface for the first 15km. Stopped for a breather in Honto (5km) where a number of pilgrims were joining the route from a small refugio there.

Met an English group of three, (father, son-in-law and daughter) from Somerset, a Spanish/American of 76 who was carrying two packs, one on his back and one on his front! He seemed to be pretty tired and did not look as if he would get very far. Also a number of French and Spanish pilgrims. I seemed to be walking faster than most. I was amazed that my pack did not seem too bad.

Always upward. Saw a golden eagle just above my head and, at one point, fifteen buzzards in one valley.

Just after I left the road onto the track at Col de Bentarte, I got terrible cramp in my thighs and thought that I might have to give up. Thought that I had made a mistake in trying to do too much too soon. I did some stretching exercises and drank a lot of water and it eased off, thank goodness. Walked on to the summit of the Col de Lepoeder and had my picnic of a baguette and fruit. Just as I finished, a huge cloud appeared and there was a spectacular thunderstorm. I put on waterproofs for the first time. They worked well but water did get into my rucksack.

The descent to Roncesvalles was very tricky. The rain on the warm ground had created a thick mist and I could only see a few yards in front of me. It was very difficult to follow the very steep and winding path down to Ibaneta. There is

*The way into St. Jean from the east. The entrance to the citadelle.*

*Looking down the Rue de la Citadelle (B&B on the left).*

*The western town gateway on the way out of St. Jean.*

a relatively modern chapel here on the site of the old ruined chapel of Charlemagne and this is the site of the death of Roland in 778. Just incredible that today I have followed in the footsteps of Charlemagne.

The last 3km down to Roncesvalles was relatively easy. The mist had cleared and I could see the abbey roof. Finally walked into the back of the abbey at about 3.15pm. Not bad going, 26km and up to 1,440m and down again.

I had intended to stay at the refugio but about sixty or so pilgrims already queuing and every one pretty wet and many more arriving to start their pilgrimage from here. I decided that I was so tired and cramped that a hot bath was the first priority!

Managed to get the last room at the Posada Hotel with a bath. Never has a hot bath seemed so good!! Washed my wet/sweaty clothes but the radiators are not working so I am not sure if they will dry.

I had a short rest then got my pilgrim passport stamped at the abbey and went to the pilgrim's mass. The beautiful church was very moving and atmospheric. I really feel part of something special.

The rather damp and misty evening emphasised the Gothic atmosphere of Roncesvalles. I visited the pilgrim museum and the 12th century 'Silo de Charlemagne', a burial place of monks and villagers of that time. I had an excellent dinner in the hotel. Fish soup, sole meuniere and rice pudding washed down with a bottle of local Navarra Chardonnay. Nice old beamed dining room and a pretty waitress.

Felt pretty mellow having drunk three quarters of the bottle of wine, so studied my dictionary/phrase book and managed to come out with "Aprendar espagnole fundamental e te quiero amor" (I have learned basic Spanish and I think I love you) which made the waitress laugh and earned me a free liqueur! Should sleep well. Radiators came on at 7.30pm so clothes are drying well.

Well I made the first day and, by all accounts, if I can manage that I shouldn't have any real problems doing the rest. It was a great experience and really glad I did it. A nice sense of achievement and now a real anticipation of what is to come.

Talking to one or two people, it does seem that refugios are going to be very full and only the early birds will get places in the smaller ones. I think, given the very low costs, that I will opt to stay in small hotels, pensions, or bars, probably with a private bath or shower. This means I can start later in the day and not put myself under pressure and be sure of a bed at the end of the day! Purist pilgrims may not see this as being in the true spirit of the Camino but for me it makes good sense.

# 17th of May, Saturday.
# Roncesvalles to Zubiri. 22km.

I did sleep well. Woke to the sound of a large number of pilgrims setting off from the refugio at about 7.00am. All rather crowded and noisy. Had a quiet, late breakfast at 8.30am and set off at about nine when the crowd had gone. A beautiful day and lovely countryside but quite a walk.

It started out deceptively straightforward with nice flat walking as far as Burguete (3km), through woods and very green fields, with lots of pretty brown cows, then quite a long steep climb up to about 500m. (nothing like yesterday) but much hotter.

Walked through other small villages, Espinal and Viskarret but the 10km walk down to Zubiri was a killer. Very steep and very rough, seemed to be walking down a dried riverbed full of boulders. Really felt my feet, ankles and thighs being tested. I'm glad I've got good boots. If yesterday was about heart and lungs, today was about feet, legs and shoulders!

Very glad that I had booked the hostelaria in Zubiri ahead by phone as everywhere in Zubiri was full. People getting quite agitated because there were no refugio beds or rooms available and they were having to walk on towards Pamplona or back down the road to previous villages.

A charming rustic hotel with a bath (thank God), I could hardly move this evening, much worse than yesterday. Zubiri is a mixture of very old and new buildings but overshadowed by the large magnetite plant. Walked up to and over the beautiful Roman bridge and watched a pilgrim with a donkey camped below the bridge. I wonder if he's going all the way? I sat for a while with a couple of German pilgrims and had a beer and a conversation in Spanish, French and German (no English).

The restaurant at the hotel was excellent again. White Navarra asparagus (a speciality of the area), scallopina with plum sauce and raisins and vegetables followed by cheese.

Tomorrow should be a bit easier but perhaps a bit dull. It is about 22km to Pamplona. Shouldn't need to book ahead because there is plenty of accommodation there. Having seen the restricted space in refugios, I will definitely stick to small hotels and B&B's.

*The Abbey at Roncesvalles.*

*The Silo de Charlemagne.*

# 18th of May, Sunday
# Zubiri to Pamplona. 23km.

I had a good breakfast and set off for Pamplona at about 8.15am. Very quiet, no sign of other pilgrims. The first half-hour was walking around and alongside the huge magnetite plant. Not up to previous scenery!

Caught up with an English lady called Susan and walked with her for the rest of the day.

I had seen her on the first day on the Col de Lepoedor walking with another younger girl and had said hello. I had assumed that they were friends but that was not the case, they had met by chance at the airport and started walking together, but Mary had developed very bad blisters and stayed in Viskarret.

Susan turned out to be very interesting. She is obviously a very clever and educated lady, an experienced walker and celebrating her 50th birthday next week. Twice divorced with three children and a career and she has recently moved to North Yorkshire from the Thames Valley. She was on the Camino to find her inner peace and joy and try to decide if she should marry her current partner. She was very clear and perceptive about changing circumstances and relationships and the need to find oneself, follow instincts and needs and accept the consequences of ones decisions.

A very intense and interesting discussion helped to pass a relatively easy and somewhat less interesting walk into Pamplona. The refugios again were full. We both opted for the La Perla Hotel where Hemingway had stayed. A bit spartan but clean and atmospheric. Had drinks in the Plaza del Castillo. Susan introduced me to 'Pacharan', a sloe based drink that was very pleasant! Dined on very good fish soup and trout with ham in a local restaurant.

Susan was a good companion and we shared a good deal of our innermost thoughts in a way that is somehow easier with strangers, one of the side benefits of Camino friendships.

A very agreeable day. Strange to meet with someone so soon who very clearly understood my situation and had the experience and intelligence to talk about it so cogently. Quite cathartic and also helped me to get some perspectives and ideas to explore further during the pilgrimage.

It would, perhaps, have been possible to develop a closer relationship with Susan and we might have teamed up to walk the Camino together. Then again, the need for personal space, the freedom to set ones own pace, is an important part of this adventure. Susan naturally wants to spend tomorrow in Pamplona, but having already explored it a few days ago, I have decided to walk on. For me, this is the right pattern for the walk. Make my own decisions, walk alone most of the time, but spend time with interesting company when and if it seems appropriate.

*Navarra countryside.*

*Bridge at Zubiri.*

*Bernhard and Igor camped at Zubiri.*

*Hostelaria at Zubiri.*

*Hemingway's Hotel in Pamplona.*

# 19th of May, Monday.
# Pamplona to Punte la Reina.
# 22km.

Left for Punte la Reina at about 8.30am. Knocked on Susan's door and said 'adios'. Bought oranges and water at a local shop and walked out of the city. Very clear marking. Mountain ridge ahead lined with windmills. It was a long, steep climb, but at the top a surprise!

An Englishman, John, with a camper van, dispensing coffee and foot treatment against a backdrop of great scenery and a clever sculpture of a pilgrim caravan. Had a coffee and a chat with John, a rather disaffected man, he said he was divorced, poor and working voluntarily for Les Amis St. Jacques, helping pilgrims in difficulty. Found out later he was a rather controversial figure as he charged pilgrims for their coffee/tea and was not officially recognised by Les Amis. Also met briefly another Englishman, Philip, who was having his awful blisters tended. I am very pleased with my choice of boots and socks, no problem so far.

It was a steep downhill descent from the ridge. Not too arduous a day but still ready for a hot bath.

Thought I might try the refugio tonight but it was very dark and gloomy and very busy. Found a Chateau & Relais called Maison de Pelegrinos, a beautiful and very tranquil old building full of antiquities and curios. I think I'm the only guest. A very comfortable room. Dining room and menu look superb but unfortunately closed! I had dinner at the next-door bar. Met and talked with a young Dutch businessman importing and exporting china and glass throughout Europe. He was totally unaware of the Camino and amazed that I was doing it.

Had a walk round Punte la Reina and over the beautiful mediaeval bridge built for the pilgrims in the 11th century. There are storks everywhere nesting on top of spires, chimneys and even pylons.

It has been good day with a mix of scenery, people and buildings. I feel as if I'm really into the pilgrimage now.

*Sculpture of Mediaeval pilgrims outlined on the ridge.*

*Englishman John with camper van dispensing coffee and treatment for weary feet! (Philip with blisters in red t-shirt).*

## 20th of May, Tuesday. Punte la Reina to Estella. 22km.

Poppies, corn (green), hill villages, Maneru, Lorca, Villatuerta, birds, an eagle, old Roman bridges, horses, foals, natterjacks (noisy).

People. Three Brazilian girls, pretty and chatty. Two French ladies, a couple from Georgia, a couple from California and a couple from Paris who did part of the Camino 10 years ago. Walked a few kilometres with Philip. He is an English freelance journalist, ex BT, living and working in Brussels for the last 13 years. He has very bad blisters. I saw him yesterday on top of the ridge being tended by John.

A sad but beautiful and memorable event. Saw a man, sixty-ish, building a stone memorial dedicated to Catherine Kempster, a Canadian who was killed by a car out of control at a crossing point on the Estella road and the Camino on the 2nd of June 2002 at 4.00pm. The man, was her husband. He was a stonemason and had come over from Canada to build the memorial. Very moving and yet uplifting. Puts things into perspective!

Made Estella in good time. Stayed in Pension/Hostel St. Andreas. A bit spartan but clean and cheap in the lovely Plaza de Santiago. Ate with Philip. Omelettes and salad. Looked round the town, a lot of antique shops and a fortified church, St. Pedro de la Rua, with a magnificent doorway.

My memories of the day.

Strawberries for breakfast, poppies everywhere, the noise of natterjacks. Catherine Kempster.

Make the most of every day because you never know what is around the corner.

*Pilgrim bridge at Puente la Reina.*

*Meson de Pelegrinos Hotel. Chateau & Relais. Luxury!*

*Estella from afar.*

*North door of Church of San Pedro de la Rua. Stunning!*

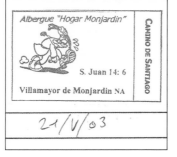

## 21st of May, Wednesday.
## Estella to Los Arcos. 20km.

Set out alone. Saw no one in front or behind for about 2.5 hours. It was a beautiful day again and glorious scenery. Huge long vistas of the mountains and the Mesa still to come.

Stopped at the wine fountain (Fuente del Vino) in Irache and filled a water bottle with wine. Saw the internet camera. If I'd known about it I could have arranged to wave to people.

Came across a mediaeval drinking well just outside Monjardin. Really felt goose bumps to think that William de Mohun would almost certainly have drunk here!

Stopped for a coffee in Villamayor de Monjardin, a beautiful hilltop village. The auberge/refugio is run by a Dutch group. Coffee was served by a young German pilgrim suffering from tendonitis. He is staying at the refugio paying his way by helping out.

Caught up with Philip again but he is still suffering with blisters and his boots and walking very slowly. Chatted for a bit and then walked on ahead. Met up

*Free wine fountain at Irache.*

*The mediaeval drinking well (restored), just before Villamayor de Monjardin. William de Mohun would probably have stopped for refreshment here in 1280. I felt that he was very close to me from this point onwards.*

with Peter, a retired vicar from Evesham. He had been in Uganda and Wolverhampton and knew Donald Marr from Cheshire/Tresco. A very nice man.

Los Arcos is so-so. Good little hotel 'Monaco' with an excellent 12 euro pilgrim meal. Brazilian girls there having fun and still very noisy.

Another good day. Interesting and involving. A long day tomorrow if I'm to reach Logrono. I estimate about nine hours walking. However there is no pressure and if it seems too long I will stop in Viana.

I have an idea forming of writing my life story matched with stages of the Camino.

ASOCIACIÓN RIOJANA DE AMIGOS DEL CAMINO DE SANTIAGO
ALBERGUE DE PEREGRINOS
Tel. 941 260 234 · LOGROÑO

## 22nd of May, Thursday.
## Los Arcos to Logrono. 28km.

Another long day's walking with some spectacular and some fairly ordinary scenery. Again fantastic weather but hotter and not so much breeze. Noticed a gradual change of terrain from cornfields to vineyards as I move from Navarra toward Rioja.

I felt great at Viana, a very attractive town with a steep climb up to the centre. Arrived at 12.30pm after a late start at about 9.00am.

Lunch outside in the narrow main streets with ham omelette and bread and 'cervesa' frio! Sat nearly opposite the church of Santa Maria with an incredible renaissance porch. The afternoon walk into Logrono was rather hot and dusty, crossing main roads and walking through the suburbs of the city.

I found a rather dingy/spartan hotel 'Isasa' in the heart of the city, but actually quite pleasant inside. Had a shower and a rest and then out to see the city. Really buzzing! Logrono is obviously a wealthy city. Nice shops, massive city square full of outside bars. Everyone is on the streets; a great atmosphere.

I am now sitting in Central Square Paseo del Espolon with gardens and fountains and the Espolon statue, drinking pacharan and watching the world go by. I need to find a Peregrino Auberge to get my pilgrim passport stamped and then have dinner. Visited the Gothic church of Santiago and saw the statue of St. James (St. Iago) the Moorslayer, quite violent!

Met up with the American couple from Georgia again, Dyna and John Kohler. They decided to do the walk when they were in Roncesvalles on their 50th birthday. Now doing the Camino to celebrate their 60th! Struggling a bit with bad feet, they had a taxi from Viana. Both teach history in Atlanta. They were fascinated with the story of William de Mohun and the 12th century Camino.

*Paseo de Espolon at the centre of Logrono with the statue. Lovely*
*gardens with outside cafes and restaurants. A great place to sit and*
*watch the world go by.*

*Gothic church of Santiago with the famous statue of 'Santiago Matamoros' St. James the Moorslayer! Echoes of the past and reminder of the present. The price of faith!*

My right shin is playing up a bit and feels rather sore. Could be tendonitis, which seems to hit a lot of people. I may need to take it easy tomorrow as it will be either 13km or 29km.

Really walked alone today, which I enjoyed and saw kites and snow on the next range of mountains. I am tired and should sleep well.

# 23rd of May, Friday.
# Logrono.

Oh dear! I have a real problem with my right shin. It is swollen and very tender. I have decided to take a rest day and see if I can get some treatment. It also gives me time to reassess the weight of my pack and have a bit of a rethink.

Had a late breakfast, checked my pack and decided to ditch my sleeping bag, a sweater and various other odds and ends. I found a post office and bought packaging, specially designed for just this purpose, packed the items and posted them to the post office in Santiago. Thank goodness for the comprehensiveness of the Confraternity booklet/guide which provides the advice and details of what to do.

I found a pharmacia (chemist), who gave me some cream for my shin and advised two days of rest! I will see what it feels like tomorrow morning, but I don't want to risk making it worse.

I bought, wrote and posted postcards while sitting in the main square, 'El Espolon'. At lunchtime I met two French/Swiss ladies who have been keeping the same pace as me. We had lunch together and I found my French better than I thought. Very enjoyable conversation. One of the ladies works in a bank, the other is a chiropodist. She also advised a second day's rest of my ankle.

Rested my foot during the afternoon, read quite a lot about Rioja and Logrono and tried to learn some more Spanish. At least Logrono is an interesting place to stay, and I am right in the centre. This evening, I will watch the world go by again in the square, have an early meal, eight thirty'ish and try to get a good nights sleep.

It has become very humid and sultry. If it is raining tomorrow I will definitely stay another day.

Spent the evening very pleasurably sampling and learning about 'tapas'. Excellent food but my judgment probably clouded by several glasses of Rioja in different bars. I like this life! The various tapas sampled included Jamon y Tinto, Jamon Iberico, Jamon Serrano, Sortida de bacatitas, Raciones and Pincho. All very tasty indeed.

Phoned home, everything seems all right. I will make a decision in the morning, re-next step.

## 24th of May, Saturday.
## Logrono.

Discretion etc. My shin still feels very sore and it is raining this morning so another day in Logrono. I need to get a new adapter/charger for my mobile phone. I left my old one in Puente le Reina. I will also attempt to find a cape as the likelihood of more rain is high and a dry rucksack and contents are imperative. I will also start to order my thoughts on writing.

Breakfast at the cafe across the street. Fresh orange juice, coffee and bocadillo jamon.

Completed shopping successfully, although the only poncho I could find was a very bright yellow. I look like a very large canary!. Rested my leg and went out to find a bar/café for lunch. The city was full of supporters of football, or torros (bullfight), not sure which. A very happy and good-natured crowd.

Storks flying down the main square.

I opted for a Greek lunch for a change! Greek salad, moussaka, baklava, wine and green tea all for 10 euros.

PM. My leg is feeling better so definitely a go for tomorrow. The aim will be to reach Najera but be prepared to stop at Navarette if the leg is a problem.

Evening food at various tapas bars. Very entertaining.

## 25th of May, Sunday.
## Logrono to Najera. 29km.

Awake early so made an early start and left the hotel at 7.00am. A rather long and boring walk out of Logrono but flat and soon got better. Walked round a big park and fishing lake and then into the hills and vineyards, vineyards, vineyards, as far as the eye could see.

I met up with a German from Ulm, he had just been walking on the coast with his Spanish girlfriend but is now on his own. I stopped with him for a coffee in Navarette then he went on. I stopped to look at a very impressive 13th century gateway to a cemetery on the way out of town and near to it was a plaque to a Belgian cyclist, Alice Graemar. She had been killed there in an accident in 1986. Made me think how many pilgrims must have perished on their way to Santiago over the centuries.

I caught up with Bernhard and Igor in difficulties trying to cross a stream where the bridge had been swept away. Lots of heaving, everyone getting wet and

Bernhard falling in the stream, but eventually Igor went across with a big rush to everyone's relief.

Caught up with two girls in their twenties, one from Florida, one from Germany and talked with them for a couple of kilometres. When we crested the hill above Najera there was a fantastic view across the plain to the Mesa. Took a photo and shared a bag of nuts with the girls. It seemed a long way into Najera although it was in sight all the time. My leg was beginning to hurt again.

Found the Hotel San Fernando by the river. Spotless but spartan as usual, only a shower, no bath!

I had a shower, dealt with my feet and ankle, swollen, but no worse. I found the Ajuntiamento and got my pilgrim passport stamped. Rested quite well despite a wedding party outside below the window with a giant drum!!

Spoke to Betty, she seems okay. She is house hunting in Nantwich with Sarah.

Had dinner across the road in a small bar. Anchovies, small stuffed peppers and a huge salad, with Rioja of course.

Altogether a good day, my shin stood up to the fairly long walk and certainly got no worse. It seemed to me perhaps, what is becoming a typical day, with beautiful countryside, interesting towns, nice people to talk to and a bit of the unexpected like Bernhard and Igor in the stream.

# 26th of May, Monday.
# Najera to Santo Domingo de la Calzada. 21km.

Easy day. Up early but late start after orange juice and coffee at the cafe. Had time to admire the huge monastery of St. Maria la Real set into the sandstone cliff. A lot of royal tombs of the kings and queens of Navarra.

Climb up out of Najera quite steep. It was sunny but quite cold. Stopped in Azofra and ordered coffee and bocadillo jamon and got half a French stick and a huge amount of Serrano ham! I ate half and kept the rest for lunch. Also bought some cherries at a shop.

Saw Bernhard and Igor again but no one else. It was very quiet and peaceful and, as usual, spectacular views.

A long straight walk into Santo Domingo de la Calzada.

I had booked into the Monasterio de la Encamacion, a Cistercian convent. Very simple basic room but with small bath and shower, no food but you can get

*All that Rioja!*

*Some other walkers on the Camino!*

*The tower of Santa Domingo Cathedral, famous for the miracle of the cock and the hen and the wayward pilgrim!*

dinner at the hotel across the road for 12 euros. I have to be in early because they shut the door at 10.30pm. I found out that this is really a holiday home for old people run by the nuns. I should feel at home!

Had a walk round the town apparently founded in 1044 by a Benedictine monk, Santo Domingo, who paved roads, built a hospital and a bridge or causeway, hence Calzada.

Also saw the cathedral and the famous tower with the live cock and hen in a cage suspended from it. All to do with a pilgrim and an innkeeper's daughter and the intervention of St. James, who saved the pilgrim after he had been hanged for having his evil way!!

27/5/2003

# 27th of May, Tuesday.
# Santo Domingo de la Calzada
# to Belorado. 22km.

An interesting coincidence at breakfast. I met with a couple from Shenstone, who know David Cox, a friend and colleague very well. They were motorcycling across Spain. Apparently they do it regularly. They were going on to Salamanca, a place that they thoroughly recommended. A fairly uneventful day. Great walking weather, sunshine, high clouds and cool. Stopped in Granon for water and to look round the church, the bell tower of which is a refugio. Came to take some photographs and thought I'd left my camera in the monastery. I telephoned the hotel to ask if they would go across the road to see if it was there. They kindly did so, but came back with the answer that it was nowhere to be seen, I emptied my rucksack and found it in my bag of socks! I had put it there for security. What a relief.

Shortly after leaving Granon, came to the border between Rioja and the region of Castille and Leon. I stopped at an information point on the border and picked up a very useful single page guide of the Camino route, broken into something like 27 sections that corresponded quite closely with my own plan. The really useful thing about it was that it not only showed the distances, but also showed, in graph form, the height in metres of the route throughout the stages. It should make it much easier for planning each day's walk.

Walked on into Belorado, a pleasant little town with a central square with a church and a couple of cafes/restaurants. Found a small hostel, just off the town centre, with a pleasant but simple bedroom and a shared bathroom. Had time to wash my clothes through and peg them outside the window to dry in the afternoon sun.

Went for an evening stroll to collect my stamp (cello) at the Ayuntiamento and met up with Susan and Jean-Claude, a rather quiet Frenchman. I had a very pleasant dinner of local trout with them both.

Unfortunately, my leg seems to be getting worse and is quite painful. I will have to take stock tomorrow morning.

# 28th of May, Wednesday.
# Belorado to Burgos. By taxi.

My leg was very painful this morning, so I had to make some decisions. I decided to take a taxi for the rather long, and apparently tedious road into Burgos, where I intend to find a hospital to look at my leg.

At breakfast at the cafe in the square, I met a Dutch couple and the woman Stella, I think, had last year, been on a three-week Spanish course in Salamanca and thought it was fantastic. Something seems to be pointing me in that direction!

The cafe bar where I had breakfast, turned out to be a taxi centre, so I negotiated for a taxi to take me into Burgos via San Juan de Ortega.

The stretch from Belorado to San Juan, mainly through pine forest, was rather dull but worth it to see the tiny but beautiful pilgrim church of St. Nicholas, and the monastery. It seemed as though there were a number of pilgrims hoping to stay at the rather small refugio here. I was glad to have my taxi.

If I had to miss any part of the walk then the long hike of something like 25km through the outskirts of Burgos into the city was it. Very boring and along the busy main road.

The taxi driver dropped me at the gateway to the Cathedral Plaza in Burgos. The cathedral looks fabulous, and has just been cleaned.

I checked into a very pleasant hotel, just the other side of the river from the main city, and got directions straight away to the nearest hospital. I walked there and presented my E11 paper, and waited about 1.5 hours. It seemed a well-organised and efficient hospital. The doctor, who spoke no English, diagnosed severe tendonitis and prescribed pills, one every 12 hours. My leg was to be bandaged from toes to knee, and no walking for three to four days!

My leg was bandaged immediately, and the pills provided at the hospital all at no cost and with very, very pleasant service. I hope the doctor means serious walking, because Burgos looks to be a city that needs to be explored. Had a very late lunch in the Cathedral Square, Plaza de St. Maria. Fish soup, asparagus omelette, wine and coffee and got talking to a Spanish walker at the next table. He had come from Iaca and joined the Camino at Logrono. He has walked all over Spain. Unprompted, he highly recommended Salamanca, as one of the places to visit in Spain. Clearly I have go to Salamanca! He was made redundant from a multinational at the age of 52. He lives in Barcelona and has a holiday house in the Pyrenees. Seems to enjoy life.

Had a late siesta and slept until seven. Phoned home. Re-bandaged my leg after a shower and went out to look around the centre of the town, a very beautiful city. Worth a revisit.

I was strolling along the river terraces and was spotted by Philip and Peter, Jim an Australian and Frances, a Canadian woman (friend of Jim). Enjoyed drinks and dinner with them, sharing a massive paella. Jim is also suffering from tendonitis. Philip and Peter have blisters, and they are resting for another day. So may well see them again tomorrow, will try to find an excursion.

Really glad to have had my leg dealt with. It was getting extremely painful and I had real doubts that I would be able to walk any further. I was very impressed with the Spanish medical facilities and the quick and efficient care that I was given.

I must try to be sensible and rest it as much as I can. I could not have chosen a better place to take a rest. Apart from missing a very boring walk into Burgos, it is also a beautiful and interesting city with lots to see.

Looking at the route ahead, it looks as though the next few days walking from Burgos are relatively level, which should help me to get fully fit before the climbing starts after Rabanal.

# 29th of May, Thursday. Burgos.

Slept like a log. Not sure if it was the tablets or the wine. Perhaps both! Had the luxury of a late start and leisurely breakfast in the hotel. Re-bandaged my leg. It felt better and the swelling has reduced.

I was a tourist for the day and explored Burgos. It is an amazing city, steeped in history. The home of El Cid. A fantastic Gothic cathedral at the centre, in Plaza de Santa Maria with its golden staircase. The beautiful church of St. Nicholas nearby. Very varied architecture, both ancient and modern. The predominant feature seems to be glass.

The fascias of most of the 3 or 4 storey buildings, comprise very tall square bay windows from top to bottom. On a day like today, bright and sunny, the whole impression is of light and space.

The El Cid memorial and the statue are both impressive as are the ancient gates to the city, particularly the Puerta de San Martin.

I also visited the Monastery de las Huelgas Reales, and the Chapter House (Cartuja de Milaflores), now a Carthusian monastery. I was lucky enough to hear the monks singing a gregorian chant. Very moving. There is just too much to take in. I will have to return!

Met Philip again by chance, shopping for his third set of boots!! We had lunch together. Omelette, salad and wine, of course.

I rested my leg for a while in the late afternoon. Wrote cards and studied the remainder of the route.

Walkabout in the evening watching the world go by, sitting by the river. Dined on a plate of tapas in a tapas bar and a very good local wine 'Reblado'. Saw various people during the evening but did not feel like joining up with a group. I would really like to press on again. I miss the daily walking routine, but will be sensible and stay on one more day and finish the tablets.

Tomorrow I will sort out my clothes again and discard all unnecessary papers, maps etc., and be ready to go early on Saturday morning.

My glasses have broken. Only a screw, I think, but will need to find an optician in the morning.

*The fabulous entrance into Burgos through the Arco de Santa Maria.*

*Recently cleaned and restored. The Gothic Cathedral of Burgos in Plaza de Santa Maria.*

30/05/2003

# 30th of May, Friday.
# Burgos.

Did not sleep well last night. It was hot, noisy and, with everything going round in my head. I need to get walking again!

Glasses mended at the second optician I found. The first said it was impossible!

Bought a pair of lightweight jeans and a sweater, not really needed but thought I might need them when I get to Santiago. Packed them up together with superfluous papers and maps etc., and posted them off to Santiago to await my arrival. Obtained my stamp (cello) at the library, otherwise it was a quiet day contemplating, planning and resting my leg as much as possible.

Enjoyed watching the preparations for the mediaeval tournament and carnival and a fantastic market in the Cathedral Plaza that opened at lunchtime.

A big parade in the evening and the whole town turned out to watch and participate. Spent too much time in and out of bars taking in the atmosphere and had a late meal of fish soup and steak.

Should be able to burn it off tomorrow!!

I have decided to get a bus out of town tomorrow morning and start walking from Tardajos. I want to get to Castrojeriz and that would mean about 38km walking which is probably pushing it for the first day back. Starting from Tardajos it will miss out the boring bit through the suburbs and will mean starting out on the meseta. It will still mean a walk of 28km but that should be fine.

Will repack tonight and be ready to go at about 8.00am.

I really enjoyed Burgos. It is definitely a place to come back to and from which to explore the region. My tendonitis problem was well timed! I just hope that it does not re-occur.

Amazing to think that El Cid had been dead for 100 years before William de Mohun came through Burgos and that nearby Atapuerca is the site of some of the earliest human settlements in Europe.

*The El Cid memorial.*

*Shady plane tree walk along the riverbank of Burgos.*

*The fabulous architecture of Burgos.*

*The way out of Burgos through Puerta St. Martins.*

3. /o5/o3

# 31st of May, Saturday.
# Burgos to Castrojeriz. Bus
# 10km, walk 29km.

I am back on the walking trail. I got an early bus to Tardajos and then off again in earnest. Very varied terrain but relatively flat as I am now on the Meseta. A fantastic sense of space, distance and light.

Highlight of the day was the Arroyo de San Bol, a delightful oasis with a tiny and very pretty refugio which supplied welcome drinks, It had a beautiful interior decorated by a female artist. At one time it had been a leper colony and a hospital for sick pilgrims. Had an unusual air of tranquillity. In the grounds is a small spring with reputed healing powers. It is said that pilgrims with foot problems who wash their feet in the fountain would have no more trouble on the Camino.

I had been a bit worried because my tendonitis, although much better, was still in evidence, so I bathed my feet in the ice cold water and said a little prayer.

Remarkably I have not felt even a twinge since then!! I hope the legend is true.

It was a long, long hike into Castrojeriz. A Roman town, reputedly founded by Julius Caesar, built around a hill with a 13th century abbey on the top. A bit like Worlds End at Llangollen. Found a nice little hostel 'Meson de Castrojeriz' after a bit of a search.

A lovely big bath. Had a long soak and a rest, got my 'cello' at the refugio and then a cold beer and a meal at the hotel. Joined a very pleasant Swiss couple, Prax and Fred for dinner. They come from near Geneva. They did the Camino 10 years ago and are redoing the stage from Burgos to Leon, but staying in hotels and having their luggage sent on every day. Fred has worked it all out with Swiss precision.

They told me that the hotel that they had wanted to stay in last night could not accommodate them as it was fully booked by an English walking group. ATG perhaps?

*The refugio at Arroyo de San Bol. Scene of my personal miracle!*

*Castrojeriz from afar. It seemed to take an age to actually get there!*

Carmen

ALBERGUE
MUNICIPAL
FROMISTA

1 /06 /03

# 1st of June, Sunday.
# Castrojeriz to Fromista. 26km.

Slept well, started out at about 9.00am after coffee at the hotel bar. Steep climb up and then a steep descent, then good straight, flat walking.

Caught up with Erika a Swedish girl and Pipi her dog. I saw her yesterday at Arroyo de San Bol. I walked with them to Fuente al Piojo. She is a free spirit, has already walked the Camino from Leon to Santiago and studied Spanish in Salamanca. This year, she was studying French for three months, but then decided to do the Camino from Le Puy. She said she was very affected by her Camino experience last year and has been walking for the last six weeks. Last week, she wished she had a dog! The next day, Pipi, the Spanish sheepdog, attached himself to her. Pipi is very intelligent. Already comes when called, and is very affectionate. She wants to take him to Sweden!! I told her to see a vet in Leon and get injections and a microchip. Otherwise, she will have no chance. A lovely girl, but I think very vulnerable.

I left her and walked on, because Pipi was tired! A beautiful walking day, sunny but a cool breeze. Met up and walked for a couple of kilometres with Jean-Paul, a Frenchman. He was wearing very light sandals because of blisters and a very gaudy bandanna on his neck. He had a huge backpack with two tin mugs that bounced up and down and made quite a racket as he walked along. He gabbled away in French. He had walked in Corsica, and the Dolomites, very good company.

The afternoon was magical. Had a picnic lunch after Boadilla del Camino then the final 6km was along the canal bank, entirely alone. Beautiful yellow water irises and an abundance of birds, reed warblers, I think and a profusion of wildflowers.

Walked into Fromista and found the Hotel San Martin, opposite the San Martin Roman Church. After changing and washing my clothes, I went to look round the church. Just an amazing example of Roman architecture. It was built in 1066 and restored in about 1900. Around the outside there are two or three hundred carved figures of animals, humans, flowers and birds stretching all around the exterior at roof level. Inside, it is plain, but very beautiful. Surprisingly, I find that it is now de-consecrated.

Obtained my cello from the parish priest and got a recommendation for a restaurant in town. Met up there again with Fred and Prax. They are a very nice couple. He worked for Swissair all his life and both are very well travelled. They have three children - two daughters and one son and seven

*The simple beauty of the Camino.*

*Magical riverbank, all to myself.*

*Yet another beautiful Roman bridge.*

grandchildren. Very open and interesting people. Obviously love their grandchildren who often stay with them, but only one at a time! They go to a health spa hotel in Austria and walk. They went there to practice for the Camino. We exchanged addresses, and they will send me details of the hotel. Apparently very informal and very good.

It was an expensive meal but very good. Fish soup and hake with garlic, and white Rioja. Will sleep like a log. . . I hope.

# 2nd of June, Monday.
# Fromista to Carrion de los
# Condes. 18km.

Shortish walk today, so started late, at about 9.15am. Walked beside the road for the first few kilometres. Then into Poblacion de Campos. I stopped there and put my rucksack on the wall, while studying the route. I suddenly felt inexplicably and compulsively drawn to the old church that was built in a hollow below the wall. I went down some steps into it and found it absolutely empty except for an undecorated alter and two very simple graves on the floor, which had swords engraved on them. I'm sure

*The innocuous building in Poblacion de Campos where I felt an
irresistible force drawing me in.*

*One of the two crusader tombs inside the church at Poblacion.*

they were Knights Templar graves, very atmospheric and raised the hairs on the back of my neck! I certainly felt some strong connection with William de Mohun.

After Poblacion was a long magical walk, again along the riverbank, to Villalcazar de Sirga. Most people walk the road route, which is very boring. The river path is overgrown in places, but with just fantastic flowers, trout in the river, frogs and warblers and so peaceful. I met two Spanish walkers halfway along resting, but otherwise saw no one!

Villalcazar had a huge church, more like a cathedral, which is being renovated. Seems that a huge amount of money is being spent on the renovation of old churches, and indeed, whole villages. In the middle of the village I found an amazing old mediaeval house, Meson de Villasirga, now a very small hotel and restaurant, sadly closed. I managed to look inside, very atmospheric.

The final leg was a rather boring road route to Carrion de los Condes. I negotiated a bargain room rate of 15 euros for the Hostel Santiago. Had big bath, double bed, very comfortable. Washed my clothes, had a good lunch at the Hostel La Corte, and then a bath and a nap.

In the evening, I toured the town and visited the main church. I bought some postcards and met Philip and two Frenchmen in the plaza and had dinner with them, also at La Corte. Lovely fresh trout.

Tomorrow a big decision. Either a short walk to Calzadilla de la Cueza or 40km to Sahagun. It will depend on the weather and how I feel.

I have felt rather tired today so early night.

## 3rd of June, Tuesday.
## Carrion de los Condes to Sahagun.
## 40km.

Well I made it! Sahagun 40km! Felt great although pretty tired at the end. Only about 6 of 50 plus who started from Carrion came all the way and all a lot younger than me.

Lovely day. Sunny with a cool breeze that made all the difference.

I had a very strong sense of walking in the footsteps of the past while walking on the old Roman road and original Camino (Camino Real). Dead straight for the first 18.5km. The first mounted pilgrims passed me on a couple of beautiful white horses. I imagine that William would have been on horseback with a small retinue.

*The Camino Real. Here since Roman times. Dead straight for 18.5km. William de Mohun would certainly have travelled on this same bit of road and I felt that he was with me here.*

Met and walked for a while with Achilles (Huerta?), a 70-year-old Brazilian who is walking very slowly but he really enjoyed talking. He had been hoping that his wife would join him in Leon but she had phoned to say that she was not well and may not make it. He said that he would probably finish in Leon. He has a daughter and granddaughter in Paris and hopes to travel on to see them. Also met up again with Stephen and the big group of Brazilians (10 of them) and the garrulous Jean-Paul. They all decided to stay at the refugio in Terradillos de los Templarios, a very small old village. I was tempted to stay but after a beer felt okay to go on to Sahagun.

Staying in a small pension with its own restaurant in the centre of town. Seems okay but not quite up to the usual standard. Sahagun used to be a major stop on the Camino, the site of the largest and most powerful Benedictine monastery in Spain. William would certainly have stayed here. Only a huge gateway arch remains.

The town now is mainly industrial and modern. Went for a beer at the very nice 'Asturcon' bar next to the pension. The barmaid spoke good English and wanted to practice it! She had been in Ireland as an au pair but it had been a bad experience. She told me that there was a famous local band in Sahagun and that they were playing outside the church that evening. I went to listen to them and they were very good, a bit like the miners brass bands in England.

Went back to the bar where the barmaid looked after me, gave me free refills and produced substantial snacks with each beer. I didn't need any dinner. Bought a CD of the band that was on sale in the bar, good saleswoman! Finished off with a Pacharan 'Zuco', which was better than in Navarra.

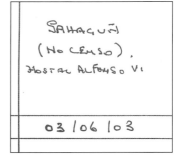

Noticed that across the road from the bar was another bar. 'Muphy's Irish Tavern'. Incongruous. Those Guinness salesmen!!

Chatted with a couple of other pilgrims at the hotel. Someone said that Igor had collapsed. I hope not. Mobile not working at all this evening apparently no coverage or it could be that O2 have cut it off because of unusual overseas usage. Phoned Betty from the hotel and asked her to check.

Very full day today. Pleased with myself for having covered the distance and still feeling great. That fountain in Arroyo de San Bol certainly worked its magic on my leg.

Really started to get into the idea for the book today. Interweaving the Mohun history and the previous Camino with my current Camino. Still need the big idea/raison d'etre to make it really come alive.

Certainly feel that the two Caminos have joined up with experiences in Poblacion and along the Camino Real.

# 4th of June, Wednesday.
# Sahagun to Mansilla de los Mulas. 37km.

Made Mansilla, 37km fairly easily. Very long straight path on the Camino Real. Along the way saw the mountains of Galicia in the distance. Things to come!

Saw Igor and Bernhard still going strong thank goodness.

Met the American couple from Georgia again. He is John Kohler, a history professor at Clayton College State University. He was very interested in my book ideas and promised to be my first customer.

Also met up with a Scotsman from Edinburgh. He worked for HBOS and had been given early retirement. He has walked from Le Puy. He says that the French end of the Camino is very different. More relaxed, more expensive and nearly all French pilgrims. Will be worth considering.

Met up in the evening in the Plaza a Mansilla with Susan and Jean Claude, who seem to have teamed up to walk together.

Turned out to be very useful as the refugio and all the hotels were full. I had tried them all and was wondering what to do. Jean Claude had heard that a lady was offering 3 rooms in a local house for 20 euros. We managed to track her down and do the deal. Otherwise I would have had to get the bus into Leon. Excellent accommodation, but no towels or sheets. I think the lady is probably the cleaner and has cashed in while the owners are away. It was also quite cold and no hot water but I managed to find the boiler in the basement and got it going.

Had a pleasant evening meal with Susan and Jean Claude. Susan now seems to be on a deadline to reach Santiago to catch a flight home. Would not tell me if she has decided to marry her partner, but I am guessing it's yes!.

Phone is still not working. Phoned Betty from the public phone in the plaza. I am right. O2 have cut it off because of high charges even though I advised them before I left that I would be using it more than usual from Spain. I will call them to complain tomorrow.

# 5th of June, Thursday.
# Mansilla de las Mulas to Leon. 18km.

Left quite early before Susan and Jean Claude were up. Had a sparse breakfast of black coffee and an orange.

Rather boring walk today of only 18km into Leon mostly along or near main roads. But quite quickly into the city centre. Arrived by midday. Walked most of the way with Juan, who had been walking with the Brazilian group and I had assumed was Brazilian. He is in fact from Madrid but works in London for IBM. He was previously in Sao Paulo and New York. He is on a sabbatical year.

He quarrelled this morning with his girlfriend and she is going into Leon by bus. He seemed a really nice chap. Shows that you should not always judge by first impressions because every time I had seen him before, he had looked very sullen and miserable, but then he had always been with his girlfriend!

Good first impressions of Leon. Smaller and busier than Logrono and Burgos and again a fantastic looking cathedral.

Found a really great small hotel close to the cathedral. An old building restored by a notable architect and called Posada Regia. Three star but still relatively inexpensive at 50 euros per night including breakfast. Also has a good restaurant attached.

After washing my clothes and a short nap explored the centre of Leon.

*Leon Cathedral.*

A stunning cathedral. Gothic, 13th Century with just amazing stained glass windows, the best I have ever seen, and sculpture to match.

Also visited the Plaza de San Marcos and went into the San Marcos Parador for a nose around. Had a drink there and used their public phone to phone home and to complain to O2.

The hotel restaurant was full! But I was given a recommendation to 'Vivaldi', which I found fairly easily down a little alleyway. A brilliant although very expensive (for Spain) meal. Never mind, excellent value.

Did not see any other pilgrims in town, but it is a very busy and lively place in the evening.

Buskers outside the hotel playing 'Cherry Blossom Pink'!!

Tomorrow I will do the tourist bit. Cathedral again, Museo, Basilica of San Isodoro, Pantheon, etc. Do some preparation for Galicia.

Thinking about a book title at dinner. 'Perigrinations around the Moon'!

Footnote. Noise all night long until after 4.00am from the street outside. I hope it is a one off but fear that in Leon every night is party night!

Did not sleep well but not too tired and I am not walking tomorrow.

# 6th of June, Friday. Leon.

Called home this morning to say 'happy birthday', flowers are ordered from Interflora.

A tourist day today, the cathedral and cathedral museum first, just fantastic. Ancient and modern designs. Joanna would love it.

The museum is stuffed with Roman and mediaeval artefacts, paintings, tombs and religious items and a huge selection of fabric designs from the 11th to the 18th century. I saw a piece from the 11th century, which looked like William Morris! It would take hours to take it all in.

The courtyard and the cloisters are divided between Roman and Gothic architecture.

Moved on, then to the Basilica de San Isodoro. According to the book, this was a compulsory stop for pilgrims. A very quiet, tranquil church, very simple compared with many and with a real atmosphere. Just sat and drank it all in for 15 minutes or so, felt very refreshed.

Then into the Pantheon Museum, attached to the basilica, just incredible! In the cloisters, the tombs of kings and queens and Napoleonic soldiers. 11th and

*Just another plaza in Leon!*

*Hostal de San Marcos, built for the Knights of Santiago, now a parador.*

12th century ceiling and wall paintings, unrestored, just as they were painted are superb, bible stories and local history scenes, early calendars showing pictorially the months of the year and what happened in them.

Also in the cloisters, the golden cockerel that used to be on the spire of the basilica. Eleventh century in origin, but with holes made by the musket balls from Napoleon's soldiers!

In the antechamber to the royal church there was a collection of relics and reliquaries and alter cups from the 10th – 16th century. Among them I noticed a Scandinavian amulet of exquisite design.

I asked the guide how it came to be there. She said that I had picked out the most unusual piece in the collection and her personal favourite.

She said that a small elite group of Vikings had joined the Christian Crusaders to fight in the Holy War against the Muslims and it was assumed that this might be the origin of the piece.

Could those Vikings be part of the legendary 'Moon Regiment' that came from Norway to Normandy and according to some took the name of Moon as their legacy. Fantastic thought!!

Satiated with culture, I had two beers and a vino tinto with the great Leon custom of side dishes with your drinks. Potato, ham, beans etc. Enough for lunch.

Siesta 3.00pm - 6.00pm, then phoned home again. No flowers had arrived!! Oh dear. But nothing I can do from here.

Lovely evening. Out again. Sitting in the Plaza St. Martin watching the world go by. Very lively and colourful. Feel a little bit lonely. Would like to share this experience.

Dined again at Vivaldi.

Marinated salmon and cheese pate,
Beans (red) in a very tangy chorizo sauce with calamares,
Filet mignon with figs and pineapple sauce & strawberry reduction (exquisite),
Flan de nata with lemon biscuit fingers and raspberry sauce.
All washed down with 'Valjunco' Rose.

Modern Nuveau, absolutely delicious, expensive but worth every euro. Tomorrow an early start for Hospital de Orbigo.

SANTUARIO
VIRGEN DEL CAMINO
PP. Dominicos (León)

7/6/03

# 7th of June, Saturday.
# Leon to Hospital de Orbigo.
# 39km.

Back on the road with a vengeance. Alright for the first 7km out of Leon along the busy high road and an industrial estate all uphill.

Stopped at Virgen Del Camino for coffee, and then to look at the great modern church with marvellous exterior sculptures of the apostles and Mary. The fresco includes St. James with his hand outstretched, pointing the way to Santiago. Dominican monks run the church. It has a very plain, but beautiful interior. Just after I had decided to take the longer country route to Hospitale de Orbigo, I suddenly developed severe cramp and pain in my left calf muscle. I sat down and drank a lot of water and a salt tablet and massaged it thoroughly, and it eased enough for me to walk on.

Would just record that this was the worst walking day so far. It was very hot and not particularly scenic. I had vestiges of cramp in my leg most of the way and the signing and distance of the route was up the creek. Instead of being 32km it turned out to be 39 to 40 and the last 10km were not enjoyable! I had plenty of stops with lots of drinks and took my time, so I was okay.

Apparently there is a mediaeval festival in the town, and I had been warned to book ahead for accommodation. However, all the central hotels and hostels were booked up, so I finished up in a roadside motel about a kilometre out of town called, bizarrely, El Kangeru Australiano.

A bit crummy but a clean bed and, more importantly, a bath with plenty of hot water. Had a long soak and relaxed.

Phoned home. Flowers had arrived, better late than never! Walked into town.

The evening made up for the day. A mediaeval festival in full swing. All in fancy dress, artisans market, and jousting, street musicians, really fantastic.

I found a restaurant/bar overlooking the puente (bridge) with Roman arches and the whole world walking over it. Had drinks on the terrace and watched the jousting and booked a table for dinner. They squeezed me in as the place was packed.

Fantastic fish soup and merluza (hake) plus Valjunco Rose, great.

Somewhat surreal surroundings with waiters and most of the guests in mediaeval costume, the view of the bridge and the jousting and a speaker system playing Irish jigs!!

Got into conversation with a Spanish family at the next table (no English). They had come from Ponferrada to see the festival. They were very intrigued by my

*The frontage of the modern church at Virgen del Camino showing
the apostles and the Virgin Mary with St. James showing the
way to Santiago.*

*The bridge in Hospital de Orbigo*
*with the mediaeval carnival in full swing.*

*More carnival scenes.*

story of an ancestor walking the Camino. They offered me accommodation in Ponferrada if I decided to stop there.

It is a nice country. Full of life and energy. Met some Americans at the refugio when getting my stamp, individually okay but collectively - Yuk! Also some Germans at the hotel, very arrogant and clannish. I am glad to be on my own and mixing with locals.

I have left Phil, Jim, Susan and Jean Claude behind now. I enjoyed Leon very much and would like to return sometime, but I am glad to be on the move again. Only 17km to Astorga tomorrow. I will probably stay there an extra day, as there is quite a lot to see.

I should sleep well tonight without the whole population of Leon passing my window between midnight and 4.00am. They certainly know how to party.

Not a good walk today but the church at Virgen del Camino and the evening in Orbigo more than made up for it.

"Es la Camino".

8/6/03

# 8th of June, Sunday.
# Hospital de Orbigo to Astorga.
# 17km.

Should have known better! Wedding party at the hotel last night carousing until the early hours but so tired that I slept through most of it!

Leisurely start, left Hospital de Orbigo at about 9.30am and took the country route again, very quiet, peaceful and panoramic views.

Legs felt rather tired after yesterday but no sign of the cramp re-occurring and only 17km to Astorga.

A magical moment. I was walking downhill through cornfields towards the village of Santibanez de Valdeiglesia. The sun was shining, frogs croaking, buzzards flying overhead and from the village church, which must have had a loudspeaker on the tower, I could hear a choir singing.

There was nobody in sight and I had the scene to myself. I felt very emotional and the beauty of it brought tears to my eyes.

It occurred to me that, apart from the loudspeaker, William de Mohun could have witnessed the same scene over 700 years ago. I wonder if it made him cry?

Walked on through gentle hills and oak woods and came out on an escarpment with a fantastic view across the valley to Astorga. The cathedral and the Gaudi Palace were clearly visible as were the Roman walls that surrounded the town. In the distance beyond, I could see the snow topped mountains of Galicia and Asturia.

It seemed a long way into Astorga. The town is set on a hill surrounded by Roman walls and you have to climb up several flights of steps to reach the top.

I walked through the main streets and plazas all lined with crowds of people obviously waiting for something (I didn't think it was for me!). I was heading for the Gaudi Hotel, which was at the far end of the town opposite the Gaudi Palace and next to the cathedral.

I checked in and had just got into my room, which overlooked the cathedral plaza and the Gaudi Palace, when there was a huge bang!!

I opened the shutters to see a magnificent procession coming from the cathedral. An army band, girls with castanets, all the town dignitaries in their robes, and platoons of men in mediaeval costumes with muskets, which they discharged in a volley every hundred paces of a slow march, as well as letting off huge explosions every couple of minutes. It was an unbelievable sight and sound show for which I had a grandstand view.

Talk about right place right time!

*Approaching Astorga.*

*Astorga central plaza with ayuntiamento (town hall).*

Had a bath and a beer and bocadillos, not ready for a big lunch. I must check if the dining room is open for dinner. Went out for a walk around. It's a lovely town. The cathedral and the Gaudi Palace are closed today. I will visit them both tomorrow. Very pleasant central plaza, great to sit and have a drink and watch the world go by. At one end there is an impressive town hall (ayuntiamento). It has a 17th-century clock on the top of the building, where, on the hour, two figures come out and strike the hour on the bell - twice! Visited some of the Roman ruins, which are spectacular. Astorga is very like Chester. Probably a little smaller, but nevertheless a very Roman town.

Sat in the square in the early evening watching the ritual Spanish promenade. It is great to see parents, children and grandparents altogether, sharing their social life, a lovely atmosphere.

What an interesting day, fantastic scenery, amazing procession, lovely architecture and atmosphere. I feel very lucky and privileged to be making this journey.

# 9th of June, Monday.
# Astorga.

A nice quiet day in Astorga, caught up with some shopping. Toothpaste, razor blades, sun lotion and postcards. Checked over the route for the last stage of the Camino through Galicia.

Met Philip again at lunchtime in the central plaza and a Canadian, Anthony Cappucitti (from an Italian family). He and his wife run the 'Little Company of Pilgrims' in Canada, he is very knowledgeable about the Camino and could be a useful reference point.

Anthony has a theory about Othello. He says Shakespeare would have known about the Camino and St. James the Moorslayer, hence the character of Iago. Make a note to reread Othello.

Spent the afternoon in the magnificent cathedral, which is 15th to 17th-century and has a very impressive front portico. It also has a museum attached with some tomb paintings dating from the 12th century. There is a figure on top of the pinnacle of the cathedral, which is that of a Maragato. The next section of the walk, will actually pass through the region known as Maragataria. The Maragatos are, apparently, a unique race and used to be the muleteers of Spain. Perhaps the equivalent of today's long-distance lorry drivers. Apparently, the villages that they live in are unique in their architectural design and I am looking forward to seeing them.

Then went on to the Gaudi Palace, more correctly known as the Palacio Episcopal. It is an extraordinary building. A huge contrast to the cathedral, built as it is, in Gothic style. The interior is just as extraordinary as, of

*The Palacio Episcopal. The Gaudi Palace. Magnifico!*

course, most of Gaudi's buildings are. It seems to be a mixture of Gothic, Art Nouveau and Rennie Mackintosh. Not sure if I like it or not, but it is certainly different.

A tapas dinner tonight, shared with Philip. Croquettas, tripe and chorizo sausage. Very tasty. Rounded off the day of with a couple of glasses of Pacharan.

Off again tomorrow, heading to the hills!

# 10th of June, Tuesday. Astorga to Rabanal del Camino. 21km.

Really nice walking. Quite hot but starting to climb into the mountains. Took it fairly slowly and stopped at Murias de Rechivaldo for coffee and then took a short detour to the Castrillo de Polvazares, a restored Maragato village. Very attractive, built in Maragato style, with first-floor balconies projecting out over the street and nearly meeting in the middle. A bit touristy.

*Walking west towards Galicia.*

*La Barraca and the Cowboy Bar in El Ganso.*

*The Benedictine monastery from the church.*

*The old church of Santa Maria in Rabanal.*

*Fellow pilgrims at the refugio in Rabanal.*

Walked on gradually climbing, and after about another 10km came to El Ganso, a small village that was reminiscent of a western town. There were two bars close together in the middle of the village. One called the Cowboy Bar and the other La Barraca. Went first into La Barraca and had a large red wine and an excellent tortilla for 1.5 euros! Then decided to move on next door to the Cowboy Bar, because it looked so eccentric. Met a couple of other pilgrims there, who recommended the meat and pepper pie, so I tried a slice together with another huge glass of red wine.

Then floated the last 7km to Rabanal. I visited the Albergue Guacelmo, run by the Confraternity of St. James and managed by an English couple. They were very busy and seemed in a bit of a flap, so I decided to look at the other small hostel in the village actually called the Hosteria Refugio although it was actually a small private hotel. Managed to get a room, the last one available, and looked out the window straight across to the church. In fact, straight into the bell tower, which I have subsequently found to peal every hour on the hour, twice, just like the clock in Astorga.

The church is run by a Benedictine mission, who conducted vespers in Latin, with a Gregorian chant thrown in. A tiny, rather dilapidated church, but packed full of pilgrims. Quite a moving experience.

Walked round the village and met up yet again with Philip and Adele, a young Canadian girl and two sisters from Los Angeles, one of whom turned out to be a film editor, who had worked on some major movies and is shortly going to Scotland to work on a documentary about the Loch Ness Monster. Very interesting. We all had dinner together.

Slept alright despite the bells. A good interesting day. It feels good to be off the mesa, and in the hills. Start climbing in earnest tomorrow.

# 11th of June, Wednesday.
# Rabanal to Molinaseca. 26km.

An early start, quick breakfast and went to church to the Lauds service and had my heart shaped stone, that Betty had found for me when we climbed Skiddaw, blessed to place on the Cruz de Ferro.

Long, long, long climb up to the Cruz de Ferro, about 5,000 feet, quite hot and I am quite pleased to have made it in one go with no stopping. I certainly feel that I'm a lot fitter than when I started.

Cruz de Ferro is a major landmark on the Camino. I think originally set up as a guide mark through the mountains. The idea is that every pilgrim brings a stone to lay on a cairn around the cross and the laying of the stone represents laying down ones burdens.

I placed my stone from Skiddaw and eight shells from Tresco, one each for the children and grandchildren. I did really feel at this point that I had shed some of my burdens and guilt.

Climbed on a little way up to the summit, fabulous views back over the mesa, but looking forward down the valley to Ponferrada, one could see some industrial haze.

On the descent there were some very picturesque Maragato villages. Obviously abandoned at one time, but now gradually being restored, as the increased popularity of the Camino brings back some prosperity.

At one of the villages called Manjarin, there is a very basic and primitive refuge run by a character called Tomas, who spends the whole year here, in what is a very isolated and windswept spot, caring for pilgrims. I stopped for a drink and a chat with a couple of pilgrims staying there and listened to a Gregorian chant being played on a very ancient gramophone.

Had a long, late lunch at El Acebo to let the midday sun pass, and after that a very steep descent to Molinaseca. I decided to stay at the Hostel Alessio, on the river by the Roman bridge. Ponferrada looks too industrial to stay in, but I will walk through tomorrow because there are places there that are worth seeing.

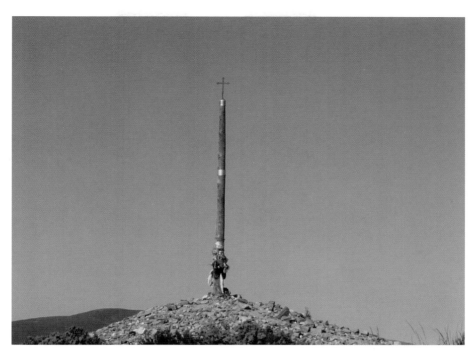

*The Cruz de Ferro.*

*The view towards Ponferrada from the Montes de Leon.*

*I have laid down my burden at the Cruz de Ferro.*
*Will I walk now with a lighter step?*

*Maragato village. Big doors for their mules.*

*The bridge at Molinaseca.*

Had a very comfortable nice bath, but poor food. No pilgrims staying here. Quite nice to be on my own again, with time to think. Went for a walk round the town, sat out watching them damming the river under the Roman bridge with a bulldozer, just pushing up stones and boulders to create a swimming pool for the summer. Great idea.

Well that was the second big climb out of the way. Apparently the highest point on the whole Camino. Certainly didn't seem as difficult as the first climb over the Pyrenees. I enjoyed the ritual of laying the stones at the Cruz de Ferro. The size of the cairn makes one realise how many pilgrims have trodden this route in comparatively recent times.

I wonder if William came over this same Roman bridge, Punte de Peregrinos, that I am looking over from my room. I guess he did. Was he walking or riding?

# 12th of June, Thursday. Molinaseca to Villafranca de Bierzo. 30km.

I will start with the end. Another magic moment !

I am sitting in the courtyard of the Convent/Hostelaria St. Nicholas, a beautiful building. I am having dinner and am the solitary guest. Sitting outside in a courtyard with lovely music playing. The menu is trout soup with chorizo, grilled meats with chips and a hot tomato/tabasco (peregrino) sauce, washed down with the vino del casa. A great atmosphere and ambience.

I do not understand why everyone else seems to congregate in some of the rather boring bars eating the menu del dia at 9 euros when, with a little bit of adventure, they could be here dining in style and difference for 11 euros. Terrific value.

It has been a long hot day. And an uphill grind into Ponferrada, which was not very inviting at first sight, certainly the most modern/industrial town to date. However I found my way to the old town and had a very nice cup of coffee in the Plaza Ayuntiamento (17th century architecture).

Then just round the corner found the Castillo de Los Templaros, the embodiment of a mediaeval Knights Templar castle. Absolutely huge and stunning despite being surrounded by modern buildings and looking across the river to slag heaps. The castle dates back to the 12th century and would almost certainly have been a resting point for William.

Long and rather dreary walk out of Ponferrada past the slag heaps and railway yards and then into a sort of garden suburb with very Scottish style houses and gardens.

*The Knights Templar Castle at Ponferrada.*

Very hot walking. Stopped off in Cacabelos to visit an interesting building, which retails the local speciality of fruit in wine (Prado A Tope).

The wine of this whole area of Bierzo is reputedly very good.

Because the shop/production plant/restaurant is a restoration of an old pilgrim hospital, I was given a free drink and tapas!

Finally, feeling very hot and travel worn, descended to Villafranca. Quite a big town but very attractive, straggling along the river valley. A very impressive Santiago church, accepted as a pilgrims final destination for those who might feel unable to make the steep climb up to O' Cebreiro and on through Galicia.

Next to the church is the famed refugio of Jesus Jato and his family who devote their lives to the pilgrim cause. An idiosyncratic refuge where one can experience a 'queimada'. Apparently a mystical experience that involves the drinking of a secret concoction and listening to tales and incantations.

I am afraid I was not tempted!

Found a small hotel just off the main square, Hotel San Fransisco. Very friendly owners and a very small but comfortable room.

Explored the town and found the Convent San Nicolas for dinner.

Walking back after dinner I saw Philip and Adele in the main square and had a coffee with them. They are intending to try and make O' Cebreiro tomorrow so have to start really early. I have decided to stop tomorrow at Herrerias at a

*More of this huge impressive castle. William must have stayed here!*

*Free drinks here for pilgrims. An old San Lazaro hospital now a restaurant and retail outlet for the famous 'Prado A Tope'.*

Casa Rural so that I can tackle the steep climb up to O' Cebreiro early the following morning before it gets too hot and while I am still fresh.

Woke up at 1.00am to crashing thunder almost continuous lightning and torrential rain. Hope it passes over before morning.

# 13th of June, Friday.
# Villafranca del Bierzo to Herrerias. 21km.

The storm has passed over leaving a beautiful clear day. A good walk, starting with a fairly gradual upward climb, mainly along the old NV1 road now being made obsolete by the construction of an amazing new motorway, with huge high bridges spanning the valleys and gorges. The old road has an excellent surface still, and most of the route was close to fast flowing rivers, going down the valleys.

Met an English couple, John and Rosemary Robin. He is in his 80s, and she in her 70s. Both taking it slowly and in small stages. They did the whole Camino, some 30 years ago and are very into the spiritual aspects of the experience. Lovely people.

Also walked for some distance with a French lady, whose husband was walking more slowly behind. Her name was Jacqueline Martin. She has a son at Exeter University. She kept talking about Bolognese cooking. She did not speak any English, but we had an excellent conversation. I was amazed that my French seemed to come back to me with great ease, and I was able to communicate much better than I would have expected. We stopped for a while, so that her husband and brother could catch up, and I had a lemonade shandy with them at a bar in La Portela.

Walked on again after the drink. Very warm, it feels as though the thunderstorm may come back. Stopped for a very light lunch in Vega de Valcarce. Short and slow walk during the afternoon to Herrerias. Found the lovely hostel, Paraiso del Bierzo, one of a chain of Casas Rurale. A country finca with bedrooms including bath and TV, nice terrace with spectacular views and a bar and dining room. Lovely surroundings. Countryside and mountain are all very green, a bit like Snowdonia. I seem to be the only guest at the moment, and certainly no pilgrims, which I like. Maybe I'm becoming a bit reclusive. Pleasant bath and rest and washed some clothes and then sat on the terrace enjoying the view with a nice glass of Rosado, and some olives. A thrush singing in the tree nearby, swallows flying high, and the noise of the river in the valley below, this is definitely a place to revisit.

Seem to be a lot of locals coming into dinner. The first ones are a family in a green Peugeot 206! A small link with home.

Very interesting party arrived and sat at the next table to me on the terrace. A very good-looking girl speaking Spanish, French and English with her

American mother from Miami. Two lovely children, girl of seven and a boy of five and a Spanish boyfriend, who owns a restaurant 'Hermanos Becker' in Madrid. We talked for some time, she used to work at Sotheby's in London, but now lives and works in Madrid. They gave me the address of the restaurant with invitation to dine there, if and when I visit Madrid.

Another large party of 10 or 12 locals arrived for dinner at about 10 o'clock. This place obviously has a good reputation for its food, which was excellent.

Went to bed early, but not really tired. Didn't sleep very well, and woke before the alarm at 6.00am.

# June the 14th, Saturday. Herrerias to Triacastela. 30km.

Very early light breakfast, nobody around. Left at 7.30am for the walk/climb up to O' Cebreiro. Lovely cool morning, walked out of Herrerias past the Hospital Inglese. This place was mentioned as far back as 1178 in a papal bull, which talked about the hospital of the English. There is also a chapel here where pilgrims were buried. I can envisage William staying here, before the climb up to O' Cebreiro.

A very steep but very pleasant walk up to the top. It took about two hours to cover the 9km. Overtook a lot of pilgrims struggling with the climb on the way up. O' Cebreiro is a very tiny and ancient village. You really do seem to take a step back in time. Apparently there was a hospital here from the 11th century through to the 1850's, which was run by French monks, obviously to cater for people who had suffered on the climb up here. A very pretty and atmospheric 12th century church of Santa Maria houses a relic of a 12th century statue of the virgin, which is linked to a local miracle. I spent some time reflecting and recovering in the cool and peace of the church.

Strolled round the village and admired the fantastic views on all sides. Had a coffee and listened to some Spanish guitar music from a fellow pilgrim busking in the square.

Fortified, I made the decision to press on to Triacastela, another 20 odd kilometres. I bit off a bit more than I bargained for. It was a switchback walk at about 4,000 feet up and down about 1,000 feet at a time, and then what seemed a very, very, very long descent into Triacastela. Towards the end, I felt for the first time that my legs might not actually get me there!

Arrived, eventually, very tired at about 6.00pm, the walk had only been 30km in distance but had also included a climb up to 5,000 feet and down again, with a lot of climbing in the middle. Probably the hardest day of walking to date.

A lot of pilgrims here, and the refugios are all full. Glad I booked ahead during the day at the Hospedaje O'Novo. Very comfortable with a proper bath and a clothes line outside (23 euros).

Toufria. 14·6·03

Philip and Adele are here. Philip is awaiting the arrival of a friend from the UK, who will join him here tomorrow and walk the rest of the way to Santiago.

During the long walk today I met a Frenchman, by chance, at Alto de Poio, who had walked from Mont St. Michel via what is known as the route Anglais, through Rennes, Nantes and Burgundy to join up with the Camino Francais at St Jean-Pied-de-Port. He said that the path in France is not very well marked in comparison with Spain and that accommodation is in hotels and guesthouses but the scenery is lovely. This must have been the route taken by William de Mohun. Fascinating and inspiring. I would certainly like to attempt the French end of the route another year.

A memorable day. Strenuous walking, the serenity of O'Cebreiro, the fabulous scenery, a bit like Wales and Devon, wagtails, yellowhammers and an eagle.

The discovery of the 'Route Anglais' still being walked.

I think tomorrow I will opt for a short walk to Samos to see the monastery. It sounds amazing and I am well ahead of myself so I have the time to spare and to recover from today.

*About halfway up to O'Cebreiro.*

*O' Cebreiro listening to flamenco guitar.*

# 15th of June, Sunday.
# Triacastela to Samos. 12km.

It is a nice cool morning and I decided definitely to go to Samos and stay there. So only 11 to 12 km today.

A simply beautiful walk, probably the best to date, through the river valley. Just like Wales, a lovely wooded valley, with cultivated clearings, very small villages and farms. Lots of very large dogs, all benign. In one of the villages I was stopped by an old man, a farmer I think. He invited me into his garden and gave me a glass of wine!

No hurry today, I picnicked on oranges and goats cheese for elevenses sitting on a little bridge over a babbling stream.

Arrived in Samos at about 1.30pm. An amazing monastery, which I looked down on from the hill above the town. It looks huge. Checked into the Hostal A Veiga. Very welcoming smell of a roast lamb for Sunday lunch.

Found the very large dining room overlooking the river. Excellent food and wine. Glad I got in early at 2.00pm as it rapidly filled up with about 150 diners. Obviously a popular Sunday lunch venue.

Nice siesta and then a tour of the monastery, which opened at 4.00pm.

It is gigantic. Currently run by a handful of Benedictine monks. The tour took at least an hour and a half.

The monastery has 6th century origins but has been rebuilt many times over the years. Now the main fabric is 16th century (Gothic and Jacobean), but a disastrous fire in 1951 destroyed most of the interior which has only recently been totally restored.

Amazing cloisters on two levels with Roman and earlier walls and arches and modern frescos (copies of the originals). All very impressive but a bit too ornate for me.

Had a walk around the town. Not a lot to see. A light supper of fish soup, pasta salad and lemon mousse.

Thunder around but not a full storm. I hope we get one to clear the air. It is very humid and my clothes are not drying properly.

Will press on to Sarria tomorrow.

*Looking down on the monastery at Samos.*

*Another view of the monastery. Just 14 monks live here!*

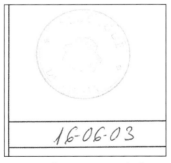

16-06-03

## 16th of June, Monday.
## Samos to Sarria. 17km.

Cool, misty, rainy morning. Needed my waterproof jacket for the first time since day one. Very light rain, actually quite pleasant walking. I felt very good after the light day yesterday and seemed to get going at a really good pace. Also nice, because very few pilgrims seem to have come via Samos. Most have gone direct to Sarria. This means that most of the group that I know will be a day ahead by now, which gives me the opportunity to meet new people. The Camino meanders through hamlets and farms. It is quite hilly but nothing too steep.

Arrived in Sarria at about 2.00pm in time for lunch. I saw a recommended hotel, Alphonso IX and decided to have lunch there, as it was only 7 euros. I had asparagus, pasta, flan, wine, water and coffee. It was so good that I decided to stay there. The rooms were very good, and also very reasonably priced.

Short siesta then went shopping for yet another memory stick for the camera.

Busy and quite modern town centre. Nothing very remarkable except for the

*All my worldly goods!*

remains of a 14th century castle and the 'penance steps' leading up to the refugio and the old town. Walked up the steps to get my cello from the refugio.

In the evening I sat out on the terrace by the river watching ducks and people. Big row between a German couple. Lots of shouting and he stalked off back to the hotel on his own.

Had a light meal in the hotel and early to bed. An interesting but uneventful day.

17·06·03

## 17th June, Tuesday.
## Sarria to Portomarin. 23km.

Quite a long climb out of Sarria starting with the 'penance steps'.

Very nearly fell badly going down a little incline after the church.

My feet went from under me and I fell backwards. My pack saved me from hurting myself too much.

Quite dull weather and not many people about. Very like Wales with grey stone houses with slate roofs, very agricultural with small farms and hamlets. The weather brightened up for the afternoon and made for very pleasant and relaxed walking.

Noticed yet another small village church being repaired by what looks like volunteer labour. It seems that a huge amount of effort and funds are currently being devoted to the renovation of cathedrals and churches across northern Spain. EU money?

The number of pilgrims suddenly seemed to increase although some of them are obviously just on a walking tour. Looked like a German version of ATG.

Long, modern bridge across the end of a reservoir leading into Portomarin and then a steep climb up to the town centre. Portomarin is a modern town built after the original village was flooded when the reservoir was constructed. However they saved the church, St. Nicholas, and it has been reconstructed stone by stone in the centre of the new town.

Refugios were full and I decided to stay at the best hotel in town, the Pousada de Portomarin. A nice room with all facilities and a view of the reservoir. Lunched on oranges and water but will have an early meal in the hotel. Good 10 euro menu including fish soup, tournados and red wine.

*Repairing a small village church.*

*A 'Horreo'. Mausoleum or what?*

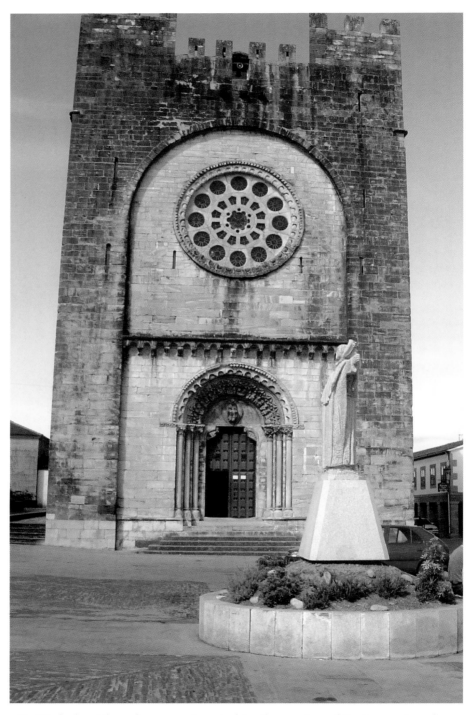

*St. Nicholas Church, reconstructed in the centre of Portomarin when the old town was flooded to make a reservoir.*

# 18th of June, Wednesday.
# Portomarin to Palas de Rei.
# 24km.

A beautiful day again, sunny but breezy. Had a pleasant breakfast in the hotel with fruit and coffee. Walked out over the bridge, and steadily uphill towards Ventas. The countryside is very similar to that I have seen over the last two days, but more pine trees and eucalyptus.

Felt very good walking today, no aches or pains anywhere. I found a great picnic spot near Ligonde, close by an amazing old stone cross with carvings top and bottom and a date of 1677 at the base, although it looks earlier. The main carving at the top is of a Madonna, carrying a baby. I sat on the bank under a very old oak tree by the cross and ate nuts and oranges and drank water. Very good feeling about the place.

Arrived at Palas de Rei, not a lot to remark on. The cafe bar 'Vilarino' had been recommended and seemed very good value at 20 euros for room and dinner.

I shared a table and dinner with a Spanish lecturer, who knows the Camino very well and was walking from Seville. He recommended Salamanca and says the ham and wine are the best in Spain. He also recommended some bars and restaurants in Santiago. I think he's in the wine business!

Apparently, it is going to be very hot tomorrow, so I should try to make an early start as the first few kilometres are quite steep.

Went to bed early but woke up about 2.00am with dogs barking and a very noisy TV set somewhere. However, a nice cool breeze.

# 19th of June, Thursday.
# Palas de Rei to Arzua. 30km.

Early start at 7.30am. A lot of pilgrims on the road. I met up quite quickly, with two Spanish girls, Visi Poente from Astorga and Harire from Barcelona. Visi who helps to run a small family hotel and restaurant, speaks good English. She had been an au pair in Clacton-on-Sea and London and has travelled in Jamaica, Canada and the USA. We were soon joined by Cisco, who is an 'Amigo de Compostela' speaks no English and two girls from Madrid, both librarians. A very animated and entertaining group. They had all started from Astorga and were on their annual holiday. I soon learned to correct some of my Spanish pronunciation! Visi and I walked ahead

*A very special place. Picnicked here in the shade of a very old oak tree contemplating the stone cross.*

*Madonna and child. The date at the foot of the cross is 1677.*

of the group, and we were so busy talking about 'Horreos'*, that we missed the direction arrow, just before Melide, and had to walk an extra 1.5km to get to the centre of the town.

*I had seen these strange ornate tomb like structures in nearly every garden that I had passed and had indeed assumed that they were family burial places, although I thought it a little macabre to have ones forebears buried in the garden. Visi laughed her head off and explained that they were simply storage places for grain and vegetables grown in the garden! They are called 'Horreos'.

We met up with the rest of the group, and some others, including one from Murcia at a famous 'pulpo' (octopus) restaurant. We all lunched on pulpo and Ribiera white wine and bread. Pulpo is obviously a great favourite in northern Spain. The octopus industry seems to have survived the 'Prestige' tanker shipwreck. I'm not too sure about pulpo. Nevertheless, I ate and drank enough to find walking in the afternoon a little more difficult!

Very, very hot, mucho calor. Visi and her friends had decided to stay at a nice albergue/refugio on the river at Ribadiso de Baixo. In some ways, I would like to have stayed with them for the company. But the dormitory was very hot and claustrophobic. Also, there was no food available on the site. I walked on another hard 3km to Arzua. It was a bit of a struggle up the hill into the town.

I found a new small pension in the main street. Blissfully cool! New bedrooms and bathroom (only shower) but very glad to stop! Met a young American couple today, briefly. He from Indianapolis, she from Chicago and also an Australian girl from Perth. All had started from Astorga and seemed amazed that I had walked from St. Jean.

Had an interesting discussion with Visi about the new type of more affluent pilgrims who want to stay in hostels/hotels with better service etc., but still do the real Camino walking. Might be scope for a new guide/directory to cater for them.

Arzua not up to much. Struggled to find a good restaurant/bar for dinner. Found one off the main plaza with pimientos padron and chiperones on the menu.

Dined with a Canadian lady, Jane Schumaker, who had been a teacher in Chiang Mai for two years about 40 years ago. She used to turn out to greet the king and his foreign guests including the Shah of Persia.

She and the children would have to bow and throw rose petals!!

Jane had suffered a bad fall and has got behind schedule. She had to skip a few sections to be able to get her flight home.

*My new found Spanish friends.*

20.06.03

## 20th of June, Friday.
## Arzua to A Rua. 17km.

I slept well, very comfortable and reasonably cool. No rush today, A Rua is only 17.5km. I got the lady at the pension to phone ahead for me, and book a room at the Hostel El Pino, which had been recommended.

Had a leisurely breakfast in the square in Arzua, orange juice and coffee and a mini-croissant.

Walked the first 8km alone, mainly through eucalyptus woods, except for meeting a couple from San Francisco and a Brazilian friend.

Met up again with Visi and her crowd at Calle and stopped for water and iced lemonade. Already very hot at 10.30am. Visi and friends seemed very pleased to see me. They said the refugio at Ribadiso had not been as good as it looked, so I am glad that I moved on.

Saw the memorial to Guillermo Watt aged 69 who died here in 1993, just a day away from Santiago! Makes you think.

Walked the next 9km with the group. Stopped again by a stream where we paddled in nice cool water. Visi and the others moving on to Arca but I stayed

*Eucalyptus woods. All over Galicia.*

*Shady glade for a picnic and cool water for tired feet.*

for a while at Santa Irena and had a bocadillo (Serrano ham). Plenty of time in hand as only another couple of kilometres to A Rua. Rested up for the heat of the day.

Hotel El Pino seems very pleasant. Obviously a popular restaurant. Room fine but very, very hot. No breeze this evening and becoming very humid, could get a storm? Not many people staying here. A French couple that I have seen en-route but I think they are travelling by car.

Well tomorrow should see me in Santiago!! I will try to start early and arrive there by midday. I will need to find a hotel and get sorted with credentials and obtaining my compostela/certificate. Then I need to collect my parcels from the post office and plan the trip to Finisterra.

No storm to keep me awake but a party going on somewhere with a very loud band playing until about 3.00am. Difficult to sleep anyway with the heat and the excitement of being so close to the end of the journey.

# 21st of June, Saturday.
# A Rua to Santiago de
# Compostela. 21km.

Well, **I made it.** I am here sitting on the steps of Santiago Cathedral in the Plaza del Obradoiro. Fantastic!!

A very happy and emotional morning. Started early and a very pleasant walk although 34 degrees at 11.00am. At first walking through eucalyptus and then on to Lavacolla, which used to be the traditional washing place for pilgrims before they entered Santiago. Now it is the site of the airport and the Camino skirts the airfield and leads rather haphazardly to Monte del Gozo, a wooded hill high above Santiago and now the site of a massive pilgrim refugio complex with room for some 3,000 pilgrims. The new facility was established in 1993 for Holy Year. Rather controversial.

Met up here with my new Spanish friends and walked the last 6 or 7km into Santiago with them. Walking downhill for a change.

The feeling on entering the Plaza del Obradoiro through the archway was extraordinary and very emotional in a way that I had not expected. I cried unashamedly with a sense of both humility and pride of achievement and sadness that it was over.

I entered the cathedral through the Portico de la Gloria, touched the Tree of Jesse and 'hugged St. James' as tradition demanded, but the cathedral was very crowded and I decided that I will come back tomorrow for the pilgrims mass, when it is quieter.

*Visi, me and Harire at Monte do Gozo*
*ready for the last leg into Santiago.*

Outside in the square I met so many others that I had met up with en-route. The hugs and kisses, handshaking, and congratulating was just amazing and the whole ambience was uniquely memorable.

I very quickly managed to obtain my compostela from the pilgrim office, very efficiently run and at a local copy shop got it laminated. Then sat at a café in the Rua de Vilar with a big group of pilgrims and drank a very welcome cerveza con limon or two or three! Other pilgrims arrived all the time to cheers and greetings. Finally at about 3.30pm went off to find a hotel for the next couple of nights. Found one tucked away but close to the centre. Okay but a bit hot and stuffy but it will do. Wrote a list of things to do, had a siesta and changed into ordinary, non-walking, clothes.

I missed the post office. Closed until Monday. I checked the booking at the Parador and arranged to check in on the 25th and to leave my luggage there if I go to Finisterra. Because of the heat, and because I cannot start until late on Monday, I think that I will go by bus at least part of the way.

*Visi, me, Harire, and Cisco. A happy band of pilgrims!*

*Santiago Cathedral. Journeys end? Not quite!*

*Party time.*

Walked around the city centre and met Philip and his friend John who had given up banking in London to become a postman in North Yorkshire! Arranged to meet them for dinner at about 8.00pm then realised that I had also agreed to meet up with Visi and her crowd at the same time. In the end I got them all together and a lively evening ensued. Lots of wine, mussels, pulpo etc., as aperitif and then dinner at an Argentinian owned restaurant, soup, tortellini, tirimasou coffee and aruco. Lots of tearful goodbyes as many people leaving for home tomorrow. Got to bed at about 2.00am, didn't sleep for a couple of hours. Very hot and so much to reflect on. Quite a day.

# 22nd of June, Sunday.
# Santiago

It has been strange not to be thinking about walking on. Went out at about 9.30am. Walked to the cathedral to attend mass and had a good look round while it was quiet.

Saw crowds gathering outside and a bishop, in all his regalia, waiting outside the Porta de la Gloria. Went and sat near the front ready for mass and then heard lots of clapping and saw flashlights everywhere. The next thing I see is the King and Queen of Spain walking by me and sitting down a couple of pews in front! Big surprise. Apparently they are in Galicia to visit the scene of the oil tanker disaster and to give thanks and encouragement to all those involved in the big clean up.

Very simple mass with a lot of newly arrived pilgrims. I was lucky because I was able to see the swinging of the massive 'botafumiero' with great clouds of incense. It needs four men on the ropes to swing it in a great arc across the trancept. It is usually only swung on St. James Day and other special feast days, but I guess royalty in attendance was a good enough reason.

Went shopping for postcards, T-shirts, souvenirs and then went for late breakfast. Met up with Philip, John and Carol. John and Carol are flying home this afternoon. We all decided to visit the Museo Peregrinacions. It was very interesting. There was quite a lot of reference to early English pilgrims with records of boats sailing from Bristol and Falmouth, including the records of some individual pilgrims. Frustratingly there was no indication of where these actual records are to be found.

I saw and talked to 'Jesus and his dog' who arrived today and Peter (the priest) who arrived three days ago but has bad tendonitis. Saw John and Dyna Kohler again, outside their hotel, they have just arrived and also feeling very emotional. They are hiring a car to go on to Finisterra on Tuesday and offered me a lift. I think I will take up the offer.

The whole spirit and atmosphere of achievement and camaraderie is amazing.

I talked to an English couple, touring by car and staying at the Parador. They were very impressed that I had walked the whole way and shook my hand. My eyes filled up. I am still feeling very emotional.

Lunched late on pimientos padron and garlic potatoes washed down with Ribiero. Then siesta and writing postcards to all and sundry just saying 'I made it'.

Saw Philip and a Belgian girl in the evening and had dinner with them.

While we were sitting out enjoying our meal there was a huge Corpus Christi procession winding its way through the city. Choir and music were relayed from the cathedral via speakers in the streets. Very atmospheric. It seems to me that the Catholic church provides everyone with entertainment as well as salvation.

*Inside the cathedral. The Botafumiero can be seen suspended by a long rope in the centre.*

*The north entrance to the cathedral.*

*The King and Queen of Spain with assorted bodyguards and onlookers.*

*The beginning of the Corpus Christi procession.*

*The beautifully decorated Corpus Christi casket*
*passing our dinner table.*

# 23rd of June, Monday.
# Santiago.

A busy morning. Went to the post office to collect my parcels from Logrono and Burgos and to post all my cards.

Bought a small rucksack for the trip to Finisterra. Repacked everything and took the big rucksack to the Parador for safe keeping. Had lunch there, a glass of wine and free canapés.

Still meeting people that I met on the route.

During the afternoon I went for a walk in the park close to my hotel. Great views of the city and the cathedral and the surrounding countryside. Also went shopping for a reunion present for Betty. I found a very pretty gold scallop shell necklace and matching earrings, which seems appropriate, and I think she will like them.

Saw Philip and had a beer with him. He is going to Finisterra today by car.

Visited the cathedral again as it was very quiet and really managed to see the detail of the Portico de la Gloria and the tree of Jesse. Just fantastic.

Had an entertaining and excellent evening meal. Sat next to a Norwegian engineer who is on holiday. Very erudite, well read, a sommelier and gourmet!

*View from the park.*

*Another aspect of the Plaza del Obradoiro from the Parador 'Hotel Reis Catolicos'.*

We got into conversation because he complimented me on the wine I had chosen (Alberino). The proprietor of the restaurant overheard us and said that the royal couple were dining just down the street and would be drinking the same wine!

At the next table were a French couple from Provence. She had been walking for two months having started from Arles and he had joined her from St. Jean. They could not speak English and the Norwegian could not speak French but nevertheless we managed to have a very convivial time and enjoyed delicious crayfish and escalope.

I need to find John and Dyna Kohler to confirm my lift to Finisterra tomorrow. I have not seen them all day. I will just go to their hotel early tomorrow morning and hope that I see them there.

**24.06.03**

# 24th of June, Tuesday.
# Santiago to Finisterra.

The plan worked. Had coffee at the bar next door to the Kohler's hotel. They appeared at about 8.30am. Seemed pleased that I was going with them. They went to visit the Museo Perigrinationes and we left for Finisterra at about 10.00am.

Quite a scenic journey. Mountains and eucalyptus trees to the coast and then a circuitous and switchback route round bays and estuaries to Finisterra. Felt a bit queasy towards the end and glad to get there. Bought them lunch, the least I could do. I really had enjoyed their company.

Went with them up to the lighthouse and the rocks at the end of the point.

Quite a sense of completion being there. Half regretted that I hadn't walked but glad that I had got there.

It was quite something to be standing at the most westerly point in Spain. I thought of those ancient pilgrims and travellers who had stood here not knowing that anything existed beyond their westerly horizon.

I burnt my handkerchief as a gesture to the old tradition of burning ones clothes here before donning new ones for the journey home. John burnt a piece of his bootlace!

Said goodbye to John and Dyna. They are driving back gradually to Pamplona in time for the Bull Run. I checked into the Hotel Finisterra, which was a bit run down, like most of the town, but quiet and clean.

Met up, inevitably, with Philip who arrived yesterday and is going on to Bilbao tomorrow. Agreed to meet him later for a beer and dinner.

Went for a long walk around the town and harbour. It could be very picturesque and there are some fantastic views, but it seems very run down and dilapidated and needs a major renovation and face lift.

Paddled on the little beach on the outskirts, so I have at least put my foot in the Atlantic.

Pleasant evening with Philip. Introduced him to Pimientos Padron and Chiperonnes and Alberino wine. We also shared an enormous paella, which we didn't need.

Last night was some sort of witch's night and there are remnants of bonfires in the streets and magic signs on pavements and doorways.

*The lighthouse at Finisterra and the last scallop shell signpost.*

*John and Dyna Kohler.*

*John Kohler burning his bootlace.*

*Standing at the end of the world!*

Obviously another all night party! Hope tonight is nice and quiet.

Well that's it really. I got back to Santiago on the bus. An entertaining and interesting trip, and checked into the Parador Hostal de los Reyes Catolicos.

A fantastic hotel and a massive contrast to the accommodation I have experienced over the last month. It is obviously spectacular, more formal and more comfortable, but in a way less interesting and less convivial.

I have a day to wait for Betty's arrival and have a conflict of emotions.

Of course I will be very glad to see her but also sad that the Camino experience is finally over. I do not think that anyone who has not actually walked the Camino can ever understand its effect. I will be able to show her some of the route and then we will visit Salamanca and return home from Madrid.

So what are my final thoughts on the Camino. Just wonderful. A true experience of all the senses, affecting mind, body and spirit.

Even as a non-Catholic, the religious aspect of the journey did have a profound affect on me. I think above all I can appreciate and marvel at the fortitude and devotion that compelled so many people from all walks of life to undertake this journey. In earlier years, particularly in mediaeval times, the danger and the hardship of the journey must have been truly daunting.

Of course, if one is cynical, the extraordinary finding of the remains of St. James, was incredibly fortunate for the Catholic Church and indeed for Northern Spain.

Whatever the truth, both believers and cynics now benefit from a wealth of religious, architectural and scenic beauty, spread across Northern Spain and a people who have not only benefited from the passing pilgrims, but also take on the responsibility for providing shelter and aid for all those who need it. I found the people all along the route to be exceptionally kind and helpful and friendly. From my own personal perspective, the experience was heightened immeasurably by the knowledge that William de Mohun, had undertaken this journey some 700 years ago.

During my family research, I had found William's old home at Mohuns Ottery in Devon, still a place of great atmosphere and beauty.

I felt very close to him throughout the journey.

There were instances, at the mediaeval watering place, the crypt at Poblacion, and along the Camino Real when I was certain he was with me and reliving his experience. Indeed I think he may have been instrumental in engaging me in the idea of this journey for some long time. As those who know me will confirm, I have had a series of experiences throughout my life, all connected with the family history and name, which are difficult to explain in any rational way. They are the subjects of another piece of writing.

Finally, I had the time and space and atmosphere to think hard about who I am and how I can move forward more positively with my life and with those I love.

Achievement.          I DID IT!

Resolutions.          Write up this diary.

                      Complete the family history.

                      Write the book.

                      Many others, but they are private!

24.06.03

William de Mohun of Mohuns Ottery
who made the pilgrimage to
Santiago de Compostela
in the year 1280 AD

William de Mohun was born in 1254 AD. He was a descendent of the De Mohun's of Dunster in Somerset who were a Norman baronial family and came to England with William the Conqueror in 1066.

His father, Reynold de Mohun the second, was a man of wealth and distinction. Apart from Dunster Castle, he had manors at Streatly in Berkshire, Tormohun (Torquay), and Whichford in Oxfordshire. He was also a zealous churchman. A great benefactor of the church, particularly the Augustinian Abbeys of Bruton and Barlynch in Somerset, he is remembered chiefly as the co-founder, with his brother William, of Newenham Abbey in Axminster, Devon.

He laid the foundation stone in 1254, the same year that William de Mohun was born, and was buried there in 1258.

There is an interesting story that, following the foundation of the abbey he attended the Papal Court of Rome, at that time held in Lyons, to ratify the consecration of the abbey. At the Court, he was awarded the great honour of 'The Golden Rose' given by the Pope to "the most valiant and honourable man in attendance at the Court."

William's mother, his father's second wife, was Isabelle de Ferrers daughter William Ferrers, Earl of Derby. She bought to the marriage a significant dowry of lands at Mildenhall in Wiltshire and a share of a great inheritance of the Marshalls, Earls of Pembroke. She died when William was only six years old.

William himself inherited a great deal of land from his mother including the manors at Mildenhall in Wiltshire, Greywell in Hampshire, lands at Sturminster

*The doorway is all that remains of Newenham Abbey today.*

114

*The site of Newenham Abbey on the outskirts of Axminster.*

Marshall in Dorset, Magor in Monmouthshire and a large estate in Kildare and Kilkenny. He also held lands from the Mohun family in Galmton, Stoke Fleming and Ottery Mohun in Devon.

There is not a lot of information available about his life but he was described as "a great soldier." In 1277 he was summoned by King Edward I to perform military service against Llewellyn, Prince of Wales. He was one of the 800 knights who marched out of Chester and succeeded in forcing Llewellyn to pay homage to the King.

Two years after this he went on The Pilgrimage to Santiago having applied for permission from the King to absent himself from service for the period. The entry in the Calendar of Patent Rolls for 1272-1281 reads "Protection with clause volumus until Michaelmas for William de Mohun, going to Santiago", dated 26th February, 1280. (You can imagine my amazement at finding this reference long after I had determined to walk the Camino myself.)

Unfortunately he did not write a diary, or if he did it did not survive. We can only surmise his likely route from other records of the time. Because his pilgrimage was undertaken before the 100 years war with France, it is likely that he would have travelled through France. There are mentions in various documents of the 'Route Anglais' running through from Cherbourg or Mont St. Michel, Rennes, Nantes, Niort and Bordeaux joining up with the Camino at St. Jean-Pied-de-Port. I am hoping to try to trace and walk this 'Route Anglais' in the next year or so and just maybe complete the whole journey.

William had built/restored his house at Ottery Mohun now Mohuns Ottery in Devon and died there in 1282, just two years after completing his pilgrimage, and was buried alongside his father in the choir of Newenham Abbey.

*Mohuns Ottery today.*

*The gateway to Mohuns Ottery with the*
*Mohun family crest on the right hand side.*

Additional notes and thoughts about
some of the practicalities for people
who might want to do
the pilgrimage themselves

1. Support and Advice

   If you think about walking the Camino yourself, join the Confraternity of St. James. They have all the resources to help you organise and plan your journey and produce the best guide available from anywhere, which is updated annually and therefore has all the latest route information. Their address is 27, Blackfriars Road, London, SE1 8NY.

   Tel. 020 7928 9988. Website – www.csj.org.uk.

   My advice is 'Do it' whatever your age or circumstances, this is a great experience that almost anyone can do. For many it is a life changing experience. At the very least it is an adventure that will provide you with happy memories and many new friends.

2. Clothing

   Buy clothing that is designed for the purpose. I chose 'Rohan' for about 90% of my clothing. It was absolutely right for my needs. Lightweight (top priority), fast drying, very comfortable and durable. Because it is made with modern technical fabrics, it is more expensive than straight cotton/wool materials but nevertheless excellent value for money.

3. Footwear

   Buy the best boots and socks that you can. They have to carry you for about 500 miles over very varied terrain and your feet need the best possible care.

   I bought a pair of 'Merrell' lightweight boots with 'Vibram' soles that were brilliant. I also had 'Coolmax' lightweight undersocks with 'Falke' walking socks with right and left feet. I never had a single blister!

   I saw so many pilgrims really crippled with blisters often wearing heavy leather boots or trainers.

4. Walking Sticks

   Most pilgrims use a stick or staff of some sort. If you want to look the part, traditional pilgrim staff's are available to buy all along the route. I bought one when I got to Santiago, to take home as a souvenir!

   The problem is that you do not need a stick all the time and if you have to carry a staff they are quite heavy and cumbersome. My recommendation is for the lightweight retractable 'Lecki' sticks. When you do not need them they can be folded up and put in/on your rucksack.

   I recommend taking two of them. I only took one and I think that if I had used two on the steep downhill sections at the beginning of the walk I would probably not have developed tendonitis.

# 5. Accommodation.

I had planned to stay mainly in refugios with occasional stops at hotels. I chose, however, very early on in the walk, to reverse that decision and stay mainly in small hotels, hostels and bars that I could reserve ahead each day when I had decided on my destination.

Purist pilgrims may frown on this, but I was very happy throughout the journey, that I had made the right decision for me. My main reasons were: –

(a) I wanted to be sure of a bed and more importantly a bath at the end of each day. Refugios are not bookable and beds are allocated on a first come first served basis. I realised this on the first day when there was a huge queue of pilgrims at Roncesvalles waiting for the refugio doors to open. I managed to get the last available room at the one hotel and many pilgrims were turned away. The next day at Zubiri the refugios and hotels were all full and some pilgrims had to walk back to the previous village or on to the next.

(b) I wanted to walk at my own pace and in my own time. For many pilgrims starting and finishing times were dictated by the opening and closing times of the refugios. There was always a big early exodus of the majority of walkers trying to ensure that they were at the front of the queue at the next refugio.

(c) Whilst I really welcomed and enjoyed the company of other pilgrims when I walked with them during the day and met up again in the evenings, I did not want to walk in or become part of a group. I needed to be free to make my own decisions about where and when to stop and to walk at my own pace.

(d) At the age of 67, I valued and needed my privacy and, it must be said, could afford the extra, albeit very modest, cost. Many pilgrims would say that there is a special camaraderie developed through sharing the communal spirit of the refugios. I am sure that this is true, but I mixed every evening with people staying in refugios and enjoyed their company and made many friends. I had no regrets however in retiring to greater comfort and privacy for my night's sleep.

List of
Hotels / Hostals / Albergues / Bars
that I stayed in with my own
star ratings.

# Rating Chart

★ = Very basic. Privacy the only benefit

★ ★ = Basic but all essential facilities (e.g.) clean bed, bath/shower, drying space

★ ★ ★ = Good facilities and services including food

★ ★ ★ ★ = Luxury

**La Posada Hotel, Roncesvalles** ★ ★
Tel. 948760225. (good restaurant)

**Hostal Zubiri, Zubiri** ★ ★
Tel.948304329. Comfortable, friendly. (good restaurant)

**Hotel La Perla, Pamplona.** ★ ★
Tel. 948227706. Hemingway atmosphere.

**Meson de Pelegrino, Puente la Reina.** ★ ★ ★ ★
Tel. 948340075. Chateau & Relaise
Stuffed with beautiful antiquities, fantastic food,
very expensive, worth it.

**Hostal san Andreas, Estella.** ★
Tel. 948554158.

**Hotel Monaco, Los Arcos.** ★
Tel. 948640000.

**Hotel Isasa, Logrono.** ★
Tel. 941256599. Very basic but central.

**Hotel san Fernando, Najera** ★ ★
Tel. 941363700. Good pilgrim menu.

**Hostal Ojarre, Belorado.** ★
Tel 947580390. Spartan, shared bathroom.

**Hotel Tryp Fernan Gonzales, Burgos.** ★ ★ ★
Tel 947209441. Very comfortable, good value,
close to the cathedral but quiet.

**Hostal el Meson, Castrojeriz.** ★ ★
Tel. 947377400. Friendly,  good food.

**Hotel St. Martin, Fromista. Next to Roman church.** ★ ★
Clean and comfortable.

**Hostal Santiago, Carrion de las Condes.** ★ ★
Tel. 927881052. Expensive.

**Hostal Alphonso VI, Sahagun.** ★ ★
Tel. 987781144. Good restaurant.

**Posada Regia, Leon.** ★ ★ ★
Tel. 987213173. Very central, very comfortable,
excellent restaurant but very noisy at night.

**Hotel Kangeru Australiano, Hospital de Orbigo.** ☆

Tel. 987389031. Not quite as bad as it sounds!
Big room, everything worked, surly service.

**Hotel Gaudi, Astorga.** ☆ ☆ ☆

Tel. 987615654. All round excellent value for money.
Great position opposite the Gaudi Palace and next to cathedral.

**Hosteria Refugio, Rabanal.** ☆ ☆

Tel. 987691274. Beware the bells! Just outside
the front windows, every hour - twice!

**Hostal el Palacio, Molinaseca.** ☆

Tel. 987453094. Quiet, comfortable and
well situated by the bridge.

**Hotel San Francisco, Villafranco del Bierzo.** ☆ ☆

Tel. 987540465. Small but comfortable, friendly owner.

**Casa Rurale, Herrerias. Recommended.** ☆ ☆ ☆

Very good value, lovely quiet, peaceful position.

**Hospedaje O'Novo, Triacastela.** ☆

Tel. 982548105. Basic but fine.

**Hostal A Viega, Samos.** ☆ ☆ ☆

Tel. 982546052. Excellent value, very large dining
room and good food especially Sunday lunch!

**Hotel Alphonso IX, Sarria.** ☆ ☆ ☆

Tel 982530005. Very good, right on the Camino.
Very good value pilgrim lunch, rooms a bit expensive.

**Posada de Portomarin, Portomarin.** ☆ ☆ ☆

Best hotel in town, good value but comparatively expensive.

**Hostal Vilarano, Palas de Rei.** ☆

Tel. 982380152. Unremarkable, but at 20 euros for room
and dinner could not complain.

**Hostal O'Pino, A Rua.** ☆ ☆

Tel. 981511148. Small, pleasant, good food.

**Hostal La Estella, Santiago.** ☆

Tel 981582796. Small room, hot and a bit stuffy. Very basic.

**Hotel Finisterra, Finisterra.** ☆

Quite modern but a bit run down.

**Parador Hostal de los Reyes Catolicos, Santiago.** ☆ ☆ ☆ ☆

Tel. 981582200. Fabulous building, perhaps the most famous
parador in Spain but indifferent service and food and very expensive.
Nevertheless a well deserved treat when the pilgrimage is over.


Finally, if you want any more information you can email me at mgmoon1@aol.com
and I will do my best to help you.